Praise for *Conjuring Harriet "Mama Moses" Tubman and the Spirits of the Underground Railroad*

"*Conjuring Harriet 'Mama Moses' Tubman and the Spirits of the Underground Railroad* represents an ambitious undertaking. It is a thorough attempt at wedding the history and legends, as well as the ethics and motivations, of the abolitionist-inspired Underground Railroad and its primary figure and force, Harriot Tubman, together with a practical system of hoodoo. As with any such attempt, it will please some more than others. It is worthy of serious consideration, as, to my knowledge, no one has attempted anything on such a scale, nor attempted to combine what is an ancestral veneration with the practice of African-American folk magic, aka hoodoo, in as much detail, ever. This book deserves to be on your reading list!"—Manuel Congo, global ethnologist and author of the *Lucumi Tarot*

"*Conjuring Harriet 'Mama Moses' Tubman and the Spirits of the Underground Railroad* is undoubtedly the most important book of the decade. Whether you read it for the history, for the conjure, or to honor the brave souls whose stories are told within . . . read it! What lies between its covers will not only enrich your life, but forever nourish your spirit."—Dorothy Morrison, author of *Utterly Wicked* and *The Craft*

"It's not often that black history and magick are given the attention and respect they deserve. *Conjuring Harriet 'Mama Moses' Tubman and the Spirits of the Underground Railroad* is an incredible work whose time has come. Witchdoctor Utu and I have been spiritual family for almost two decades. We have been together inside ritual and out, and I truly can't find enough wonderful things to say about him. His first book is stunning and not to be ignored."—Lilith Dorsey, author of *Voodoo and Afro-Caribbean Paganism* and *Love Magic*

"We are in the midst of perilous times, often mired in indecision and pessimism as we traverse a world that has become unfamiliar. *Conjuring Harriet 'Mama Moses' Tubman and the Spirits of the Underground Railroad* points out a spiritual North Star that may offer direction to your path and lift up your heart. Harriet Tubman is an elevated spirit, one of the Mighty Dead, that can be called upon and venerated, and who acts as an example for changing the world for the better. This book offers a working system that blends and acknowledges the Christian, African, and folk magic traditions that are the natural home for those called to work with Mama Moses. She does not rest in peace, she rises in power."
—Ivo Dominguez Jr., author of *Keys to Perception* and *Spirit Speak*

"I have practiced my particular brand of spirit communication for many years. During that time, I have been blessed to meet and interview several people whom I believe have left a mark on the world. Witch-doctor Utu is one such person, and he has written one of the best, well-rounded tomes on the topic in recent years. It is important that the reader grasps not just the physical practice of working with spirits but also the history behind those practices. Utu has achieved a balance seldom found. In *Conjuring Harriet 'Mama Moses' Tubman and the Spirits of the Underground Railroad*, he has married the practice of mysticism and religious belief. He also goes on to present the importance of the ancestors who brought these beliefs with them as they traveled along the Underground Railroad. Most importantly, Utu has a deep-set passion to spread the story of the life of Harriet Tubman, or Mama Moses, as she was known. Considered one of the architects of the liberation of African slaves during the time of political strife that preceded and endured during the American Civil War, her story alone is worth discovering within the pages of this book. *Conjuring Harriet 'Mama Moses' Tubman and the Spirits of the Underground Railroad* is a practical manual of instruction giving both the adept and novice fresh knowledge to add to the ever-growing need for conjure in today's world. This is a text that should grace every metaphysical worker's bookshelf." —Rev. Timothy Shaw, Spiritualist minister

"In this rich, riveting, and inspiring guide, Witchdoctor Utu opens the door to a powerhouse of spiritual help from Mama Moses and her followers. *Conjuring Harriet 'Mama Moses' Tubman and the Spirits of the Underground Railroad* is an excellent book for the true seeker who wishes to participate in the grace, beauty, and mystery at the heart of spiritual work." —Rosemary Ellen Guiley, author of *Guide to Psychic Power*

"*Conjuring Harriet 'Mama Moses' Tubman and the Spirits of the Underground Railroad* by Witchdoctor Utu is a rare and priceless literary treasure in contemporary published material on hoodoo and southern rootwork. Read this special tome—be educated, witness devotion, and be inspired by the power of this holy woman and her devoted priest, Utu. Let her spirit ignite your commitment to freedom and overcoming tyranny. *Conjuring Harriet 'Mama Moses' Tubman and the Spirits of the Underground Railroad* offers ample resources—for magic most rears its head when freedom is most oppressed." —Orion Foxwood, author of *The Candle and the Crossroads: A Book of Appalachian Conjure and Southern Root-Work* and *The Flame in the Cauldron*

"Presented in an engaging manner, Witchdoctor Utu's impressive new book, *Conjuring Harriet 'Mama Moses' Tubman and the Spirits of the Underground Railroad*, is an exercise not only in the spiritual elevation of heroic ancestors but also in the elevation of everyone who values and fights for freedom from enslavement. Utu asks us to put aside for a moment the usual history and understanding of the legendary fugitive slave turned conductor of the Underground Railroad and to focus on the empowering spiritual beliefs held by abolitionists and freedom seekers that played a vital role in their journeys to freedom. In his book, which is more than a grimoire of conjures, Witchdoctor Utu shares the rarely told stories of those who followed the North Star to freedom from the antebellum South to St. Catharines, Ontario, protective roots in hand. He brings to light a powerful conjure tradition that, with a Cairn and Cross, guides the spiritual seeker toward a meaningful way to honor Mama Moses and the spirits of the Underground Railroad and revere the bones of those still lying in unmarked graves."—Denise M. Alvarado, author of *Voodoo Hoodoo Spellbook*

Conjuring Harriet "Mama Moses" Tubman

and the Spirits

of the Underground Railroad

WITCHDOCTOR UTU

Foreword by Baba "Teddy" Olujimi Jauw

WEISER
BOOKS

This edition first published in 2019 by Weiser Books, an imprint of
Red Wheel/Weiser, LLC
With offices at:
65 Parker Street, Suite 7
Newburyport, MA 01950
www.redwheelweiser.com

ISBN: 978-1-57863-644-0
Library of Congress Cataloging-in-Publication Data available upon request.

All scripture quotes are taken from the King James Bible.
Cover and interior design by Kathryn Sky-Peck
Typeset in Adobe Caslon

Printed in Canada
MAR
10 9 8 7 6 5 4 3 2 1

Dedicated to you, Spirits of the Underground Railroad,
whose names have been forgotten, your places of rest lost to time.
May the work within these pages help bring many more friends to envelop
you in love and illumination, sustenance and elevation.
As you instructed, this work is for you. May your light shine on.

Contents

Acknowledgments

I want to thank first and foremost my family for all your love, support, and encouragement, no matter where the hand of spirit guides me. Whether here in the Americas or from home in Scotland, whether in life or my ancestors in the hereafter, I am grateful for your love.

To the New Orleans Voodoo Spiritual Temple, Priestess Miriam, and Priest Louis Martiné, the inspirations I am blessed to call clergy and blessed to continue to serve with honor: If it were not for the temple and her members including Chris, Julia, and Lilith Dorsey, I may never have heard the whispers from the spirits of the Underground Railroad, and I may never have received the light that Mama Moses can bestow. This work would not have been possible without you.

To Lady Rebecca: For the years of magic, trials, and tribulations you initiated me among, setting the tone that would enable me to follow the mysteries to the destinies that await, I am grateful. This work would not have been possible without your having been in my life and being the first priestess I served in perfect love and perfect trust.

To my Dragon Ritual Drummer brothers, from Flint in the afterlife to the ones who still drum among the living, past and present members: It was our drums on that very block at the end of the Underground Railroad that woke the spirits up from their slumber, and you have served and contributed to them and this entire tradition, receiving the light and power that has led to this book. Across North America, we have together told their stories, sung their songs, and illuminated their Cairn and Cross. No one could ever know of the adventures and manifestation we have seen while helping elevate the spirits. What we have witnessed is a mystery among brothers. Special thanks go to Alen W. Greene (Sin): It was you and I living on that very block, you and I that formed the first conjures to answer their call. To Adrian, your love, devotion, and creativity have made much of this tradition possible. To Steve Mueller, it may have been brief, but you helped us plant the seeds. Drago, what a rock and pillar you have been, a true minister for the work we have done and continue to do. Ian, music has been the reason that our fates would bring us together, and we have drunk from the chalices of rock and roll, magic, and brotherhood. Ron, my oldest friend, your creativity and talent have been a part of not only the drummers, but also the magic shared in these pages. Naresh, Brian, and Davor, my brothers, I thank you for all your contributions to the magic that we shared for the spirits across the lands, and I'm grateful for your brotherhood. It took a horde of Dragon Ritual Drummers to make this work possible, plant the cross, and share it with the world, and I love each and every one of you for it.

John Huculiak, you have been a solid part of helping me find that which needs to be found—you are corvus indeed. For the assistance with research to the books and antiquities you have given me, thank you.

Melissa Rai Duncan, when the Niagara Voodoo Shrine took root, it was our home. Your spirit, love, and blood enabled much of this magic to be nurtured and now shared. Thank you.

Lil' Jenn, for the years of love spent straddling the gateway to freedom, among the shadows of the Marble Orchard, I thank you.

To Christian Day and Brian Cain: The witchcraft that you wield from Salem to New Orleans is a direct line to how this work is now being shared, and I thank you for that.

Orion Foxwood, you showed me that this spirit world could and should be shared with the world, and I am grateful for the conjure and witchcraft we have shared, from remote crossroads to the holy grounds of Mama Moses. You have been an inspiration, teacher, and support, and I thank you.

To Denise Alvarado, I thank you for being one of the first to publish my works on Mama Moses and helping bring more light to the Underground Railroad spirits, as well as for your encouragement and support.

To Rev. Tim Shaw, Virgil Bromaghin, Mama Starr Casas, Joseph Alexander Robicheaux, Kate Russell, Papa Joe Fisher, Cat Thagard, David Lewis-Laurent, and Josh and Jamie Lee Charette : Each of you at some point enabled, inspired, supported, or revealed something that made a world of difference. Thank you so much.

To my old friend and mentor in Ifa, Prince Bamidele Bajowa, Chief Egbayelo of Osooro: For the many adventures in our time, for your blessings and encouragement toward exalting Mama Moses and all the work we did together, I thank you.

Manuel Congo, your encouragement and words of wisdom regarding the work for the spirits of the Underground Railroad are cherished, as well as the roads you have revealed that are possible. Many thanks.

Don Papson, for the encouraging words to go where few do and recognizing that this is work guided by the spirits, to you and the North Star Underground Railroad Museum, thank you.

To Baba Ted Jauw and Kate Jauw: You have both been a tremendous support and inspiration. Few people have been able to take the spirits of the Underground Railroad and their legacies and share them like you have. I am so honored to have been able to work with and learn from you.

To the trustees of the Salem Chapel, British Methodist Episcopal Church, St. Catharines: For the many years of kindness shown despite our very different cut of cloth, I thank you. Your ancestors and the house of prayer they built are an inspiration to humanity, and I always wish nothing but the best for your congregation.

To the freedom seeker descendants in St. Catharines, Niagara Region, Buxton, Chatham, Toronto, and Owen Sound, whose ancestors had to overcome so many obstacles to achieve their freedom: They are heroes, and I honor them and you. I thank you for the years of trust, gifts, stories, and friendship. As promised, I offer no first names, but honor your families for their legacy: Brady, Prince, Summers, Bell, Scott, Alexander, Dorsey, Harrison, Bush, Dawson, Woodbeck, Harper, Wilson, Marsman, Leslie, Bayliss, Morrison, Miller, Craig.

To all of the people over the years that have taken the conjures and formula and put them into practice, allowing Mama Moses and the Underground Railroad spirits to enter your lives and in turn nourished them: you have all been a part of this journey, and I thank you.

And to Judika Illes: I could never express my gratitude enough for your support, patience, and encouragement. Thank you from the bottom of my heart and soul.

Thanks also to the following:

Rick Bell Family Fonds and Collection

Lewiston Museum and Archives

First Presbyterian Church, Lewiston, New York

Carolyn Cross, B.A., M.A., Curator of Collection,
Oakville Museum Ontario

North Star Underground Railroad Museum, Ausable Chasm, New York

Uncle Toms Cabin Museum, Dresden, Ontario

Toronto Textile Museum of Canada

Grey Bruce Museum and Archives

St. Catharines Museum & Welland Canals Centre

Zion Baptist Church, St. Catharines

John W. Jones Museum, Elmira, New York

Brock University, Archives and Special Collections

Black Moon Publishing Archives

Foreword

Usually, when you read a foreword, you expect someone you know or recognize to tell you why you need to read what you are about to read. What you are about to see here is different. It is not the type of thing that you might find a famous academic or author to "forward" by penning a "foreword." So, I am going to beg your indulgence by telling you that, like Utu, I stand on the shoulders of great teachers, ancestors, and others who are a part of what you are about to read.

If they were still alive, my own teachers would probably be writing this. As experts, academics, and learned legends, they would add a certain gravitas that, I am sure, you will not get from me. As a traditional African priest and famous drummer, Babatunde Olatunji had an encyclopedic and often unwritten knowledge of African diasporic traditions, rhythms, and practices. Another personal teacher was Mary Loomis, PhD, who was a Jungian scholar and also a traditional teacher of indigenous world knowledge. They not only taught me personally, but they connected me to literally hundreds of indigenous teachers, healers, practitioners, and others who held the knowledge that informs what you are about to read about. They, and the many elders, teachers, and others who have "walked on" with this knowledge and wisdom, are who should be writing this foreword, but you are stuck with me. I will do my best, but must acknowledge their inspiration, information, and indigenous worldview that recognizes and honors what Witchdoctor Utu is doing in this book but, also and most importantly, with the whole of his being.

First, I want to suggest that what my friend Utu is revealing here is neither new nor heretical. As an Oluwo (teacher) and BabaL'Awo (priest) of traditional Yoruba Odu/Ifa, I can assure you that the elevation of heroic mortals to the level of Orisa (or Ogun or Egun, depending on the tradition) is an important part of the cultures that believe that *ori* (destiny) and *ewa* (character) are job one here on Earth and that the mark of a good life lived (*Ewa Pele*) is to be considered worthy of veneration and sacrifice. A good example is the elevation or beatification of Jakuta, third Olofin of Ile-Ife to become Shango.

As a priest of Gineh Yoruba or what some call Haitian Yoruba VoDou, I can also assure you that *elevación* is a necessary and traditional aspect of the many variants and vital facets and faces of what some generically call voodoo, which is as diverse as Christianity or Islam in its many glorious diasporic forms, practices, and terminology. While we all don't agree on everything, I believe that we all do agree that some lives are worthy of elevation and call this process by many names. That is primarily why the possibility of syncretization or saint-making/masking came about: to hide and preserve many religions in the face of Code Noir and the attempted destruction of the many traditions and paths imported with the millions of slaves ripped from a whole continent to be placed together in a New World.

Whether we exalt our heroes as saints or Orisa (Orisha, Orixa, etc.), Lwa (Loa, Lua, etc.), or something else does not matter. And while Utu himself would not want to suggest that he is applying any one specific tradition's idea of what this is and how it is done, I want to assure you, the reader, that this is a universal and important part of most indigenous and distinctly African practices that, like sainthood, is not so much for the benefit of the dead as it is for the real recipients of this practice.

Harriet Tubman has fulfilled her destiny, and I can tell you with complete certainty that she is unimpressed, unmoved, and unchanged by our elevating her to some exalted position she never sought while living and won't buy her a cup of coffee where she is now. Elevation is for the living. It is for us. And that is why I support what my brother Utu is doing here. I also think that to avoid confusion or controversy, we need to look at this type of elevation not as belonging to any specific religion or tradition but as a more universal and archetypal illumination that is not meant to deify anyone but to uplift them and their memory in our hearts and minds and diverse practices. By lifting up those who have gone before us and holding up their lives, loves, and legacy as a focus for veneration, sacrifice, and divination, we are not just upholding and evolving ancient traditions but—and more importantly—lifting up ourselves in a world that needs serious uplifting. And there are few who are as worthy and as relevant as Harriet Tubman for her ability to elevate and inspire us. I'm not creating an analogy or metaphor here, and neither is Utu.

The need to revive an Underground Railroad is more important now than ever. The need to self-identify as conductors and engineers in modern times cannot be overestimated. To be succinct, there are more literal and actual slaves today than in all of the five hundred years of Middle Passage slavery combined. Beyond *actual* slavery at well over forty-five million, there is also the specter of every other type of metaphorical slavery under the sun. And many of us are beginning to realize that we ourselves are enslaved and just didn't know it or were in denial.

And for those of us who have liberated ourselves or were privileged enough to never have been enslaved either literally or metaphorically, there is an even more important aspect of elevation than crossing our own private River Jordans. The true underlying point of elevating General "Mama Moses" Tubman is not that she escaped to freedom but that she crossed the river back again repeatedly to relentlessly rescue others. When

I say that she is relevant, I mean that she relieves something, and if we are actually elevating ourselves, it needs to be beyond our own freedom and our own salvation. We elevate a person to emulate that person. . . . Now more than ever, we need to cross the river to freedom, but we also must cross that river time and again to go get everyone who remains in whatever bondage they are in. *No one is free until everyone is free.*

So, if you are reading this book to get some information without understanding the underlying reason *why* a witchdoctor from Scotland is doing this, then you are missing an essential point. I want to make sure that this foreword will direct you to the True North of what my friend Utu is sharing and what he lives. This is a *call to action*. In that sense, I want to tell you that this is not the kind of book that you will find being vetted by academics, religious leaders, or famous authors who prescribe or proscribe specific religions or paths. Instead, I want to suggest to you that this is something that you may want to read in an open and receptive way because it is not a reference book to refer to but a *tale to be told and to unfold* inside of you however it needs to. In that way, we see Utu is actually much closer to the tradition of griot messenger or Elegbara, the wandering messenger and rogue bardic priest.

I once asked a famous and wise Native American medicine man how I could become his apprentice. He told me that he no longer teaches people to pass on what he has preserved. He told me that the medicine man of today is not the teacher, the preacher, the shaman, the priest, or even the pope. The medicine men of today are the storytellers, artists, and musicians changing the world. For it is only they who can affect the collective consciousness while those others mentioned are consciously or unconsciously holding us back or, worse, separating us from each other.

If that is true, and I believe it is, then Utu is all of those things and this book: this telling represents more than simply what is *true* but is what is *truth*. So please take what he has written not simply to learn (although you will learn a lot), but mostly to remember and to elevate yourself.

Finally, what the good doctor Utu has done here is also like an illumination—like you might see in *The Book of Kells* or an ancient single letter drawn by a devotee's own artistic hand. While intricate and beautiful, it is truly only the first letter in a sentence, paragraph, or book, and that is the part that is yours as you read this and it inspires you to illuminate, elevate, and ignite your own reason to cross the river, whether it is to freedom or back to free those still enslaved. The Railroad still goes both ways. . . . S'Alaafia ni!

—Baba "Teddy" Olujimi Jauw

Introduction

When you think about the Underground Railroad, what images come to mind? Do you see mysterious lanterns illuminating dark forest paths? Do you picture quilts hanging at Quaker homes with codes and clues for the weary freedom seeker? Is it the North Star guiding travelers on a clear night? Do you think of the Underground Railroad's most famous and celebrated conductor, Harriet Tubman? Or perhaps you're familiar with the name but don't really know much beyond that.

The Underground Railroad (or as we abbreviate it in my tradition, the U.G.R.R.) was a series of networks, secret trails, and safe houses that existed in the United States during the early to mid nineteenth century. Funded and supported by abolitionists, it was designed to aid freedom-seeking runaways fleeing slavery. While abolitionists were predominantly white freethinkers, many "free people of color" were also dedicated to the cause. Although most of the routes and tracks of freedom ran north and into Canada—most notably to Ontario—there were also routes that at times ran south into Florida and on to the Caribbean as well as others leading west. The height of this clandestine and illegal movement was around 1840–60.

There was truly no "underground" nor any "railroad," at least not in a literal sense. Hidden meaning and code were the norm and necessity for a movement funneling escaped slaves to freedom. The term "underground" applied to its clandestine purpose: it was a secret—albeit the worst one kept eventually—yet it still was never compromised as a whole. "Railroad" described a means to travel, and while there were times actual railroad lines were used, it was not what the term referred to. However, railroad terminology was employed for much of the U.G.R.R. code to describe routes and safe locations: people that helped run the trails were "conductors," places that were safe to stay were "stations," runaways were "baggage," and those that housed runaways were "station masters."

A loosely connected entity of this nature was an expensive one to maintain. There needed to be money for food, clothing, and supplies, as well as to pay for intelligence and at times even bribes. Not that every single person who traveled on the U.G.R.R. was able to benefit from the funded lines to freedom, not even close, but it still took immense support from various abolitionist societies for supplies, news, and awareness to reign. The truth is an overwhelming number of runaways traveled to freedom by themselves, through hostile swamp and marsh, with little support other than their will, their courage, and the love of their ancestors.

It never ceases to amaze me how far ahead of its time the U.G.R.R. was in many ways, that such a network and movement would exist in the 1800s, in a time when institutional slavery was legal in America. That so many men and women of every creed and color would not only stand for what is right, what is just, but would do so at the risk and peril of their livelihood, freedom, and sometimes even their own lives is such a profound, sacred, and inspiring reality. In these modern times we could certainly learn a thing or two from that sort of community that crossed religious, economic, and racial lines. As this book will demonstrate, not only is the U.G.R.R. an inspiring entity to draw from, but so too is the spirit world it frames, a spirit world that uplifts us as we nurture them in reciprocity. In gratitude, hand in hand we can become illuminated, healed, and in turn continue to bring light and reverence to this legacy.

The Americas have a dark history at their foundation. While new nations were built under a pretense of freedom and equality, they were done so by not only displacing the indigenous peoples of the Americas in genocidal proportions, but also enlisting the horrendous trade of human slavery. The level of cruelty, pain, and suffering of the African slave trade in the Americas set a standard so terrible that to this day it still reverberates. In many ways, North America has not come to terms even now with the horrendous treatment of indigenous peoples nor the brutal enslavement of the Africans. This legacy is something that we continue to strive to heal and solve in our complex modern society. We cannot be naive to the fact that many of the African traditional religions (ATRs) that have proliferated and become attractive and exotic forms of spirituality to many in North America are a direct product of the will to survive, be free, and maintain dignity in the face of the subhuman treatment of slavery. We cannot drink from the cup of conjure nor read from the bones of rootwork without fully knowing what those legacies stand for and how they had to adapt to institutional genocide, rape, murder, and enslavement. ATRs and spiritual expressions such as vodou and Santeria, as well as American conjure, hoodoo, and rootwork, are all traditions that are based in the struggle against the North American slave trade by those who were in its bondage.

The Underground Railroad was one of those traditions, but one with a slightly different foundation than most ATRs and their spirit worlds. The U.G.R.R. was a movement and fight against slavery engaged in by people of many colors, many classes, and many religions. An entire continent was divided when it came to slavery, and it's safe to say that those who fought for and maintained the U.G.R.R. and all that it stood for were on the right side of history, the just side with regard to human dignity and freedom.

The U.G.R.R. is often misunderstood, and at times romanticized with falsities from white American and Christian narratives. There is not much we can do about that except to shed light upon the truths and realities of what the U.G.R.R. was before we can delve into the actual rich and colorful spirit world it houses. Bear in mind that entire books and volumes have and will continue to be written about the U.G.R.R. in academia, so it's not realistic that this book—a grimoire of conjures and magic housed within mysteries pertaining to the U.G.R.R.—can be one of them. But we will touch upon many legacies, histories, and realities, as well as the spiritual blood, sweat, and tears behind the movement.

One truth not commonly discussed in the mainstream narrative is that many abolitionists' beliefs were rooted in controversial forms of spirituality or a lack thereof. Notable abolitionists were immersed in mysticism, spiritualism, mesmerism, the occult, and atheism. The fact that so many abolitionists and those that supported the movement were steeped in alternative forms of spirituality is uniquely responsible for practices that are a cross-pollination of Quaker mystics and runaway slaves, of whom many were adherents of conjure and rootwork. The fact that up to 100,000 escapees from slavery traveled north via the U.G.R.R., with their many forms of spirituality including Christianity, voodoo, conjure, and rootwork, and who in turn broke bread and intermingled their practices with some of their Quaker hosts, is an example of the sheer progressive and esoteric nature of the U.G.R.R. Rootwork, mysticism, and animism are all significant parts of the U.G.R.R. The trails and routes of freedom were saturated in magic, spells, and ancestral veneration. The safe houses were breeding grounds of religious fraternity. The means and ways of codes, signals, and terminology that defined the U.G.R.R. were equal parts Christian, Jewish, and African, intermixed into a formidable formula that would challenge a very society built upon injustice and in many ways would contribute to the defeat of the tyranny of slavery. However, over the years, "alternative spirituality"—be it African traditions, Christian mysticism, or combinations of the two—has been left out of the histories as a paramount piece of the wheel that helped the freedom train run.

In the same way, the reality of how many slave revolts and battles for freedom took place—many empowered again by African traditions, Christian mysticism, or the combination of the two—is hidden away in favor of a more romantic and peaceful image of the U.G.R.R. This is not only tragic, but a falsity. The unique collaboration of the U.G.R.R. was not devoid of blood spilled on its trails—far from it. Many of the white supporters of the U.G.R.R. were radicals who took the lives of slavers and bounty hunters in retribution for their bad acts. As well, many of the enslaved, whether by revolt or in self-defense on the trails of freedom, also spilled a river of blood. The reality of what the U.G.R.R. was remains complex. Yes, kind Quakers hid runaway slaves in their barns and properties. Yes, white men and women of high society funded the movement philanthropically. And yes, many of the runaways and their supporters were God-fearing folk. But it is also true that many traveling on the railroad were fierce warriors and African shamans and many of the white supporters were radical insurrectionists. The safe houses were also places where spirits were invoked, fed, and empowered. The celebrated Harriet Tubman, whom so many recall as a devout Christian of a gentle nature, was at the same time a gun-toting conjure woman, by all accounts not afraid to use her "piece," whether on slavers, their hounds, or the wavering traveler on her track—one who considered running back to the plantation, thus risking the rest of the group.

I live in St. Catharines in Ontario—the very town where Harriet Tubman brought her particular "track" of the Underground Railroad to its end. Living in St. Catharines—a stone's throw from the very buildings in which she lived, planned, prayed, and made decisions that would change history—gives me a unique perspective. The old neighborhood that was once called many things—"colored town," "free town," and "little Africa"—still remains, but it's a ghost of itself these days—with an emphasis on *ghost*. The spirits of many freedom seekers still haunt this area, as well as spirits making spectral pilgrimage to the still standing and functioning house of prayer that Harriet Tubman attended: the British Methodist Episcopal (BME) Church.

At the center of a two-block neighborhood, the BME Church is still operated by the descendants of freedom seekers and served by a congregation of descendants too, albeit a small flock. A few of the original buildings from that era still stand, built by the hands of runaways, as does another historic house of prayer in the Zion Baptist Church just up the street. There too are actual bodies laying in unmarked graves in the 'hood in what were once graveyards, old boneyards for incredible humans that walked from as far away as the Gulf of Mexico to right here in the Niagara Region where St. Catharines is located—a few are now laying under a parking lot, an empty plot, and a backyard or two. Yes, the old 'hood is sadly barren. But here in St. Catharines, in the lonely block that is the veritable end of the U.G.R.R., the North Star still shines down a sacred column of light upon the "Promised Land." Spirits still inhabit the moonlit streets that were once impenetrable. No white man could enter this area back in the day unless he was a "friend" or known to the residents. Plain and simple, bounty hunters did try to come and recapture escapees, but most never returned and some literally lost their heads and were scattered. You won't find that reality in history books, nor mention of this neighborhood, let alone St. Catharines, in many "respected" historical writings from a U.S. perspective. The legendary John Brown, a holy man and the U.G.R.R.'s most radical abolishionist, who came to St. Catharines for his fateful few weeks with Tubman, had to wait nearly four days at a saloon uptown till an emissary was sent to bring him and his entourage to Mama Moses and her enclave. It was sometimes like the Wild West in these now ghost-ridden streets.

For the better part of twenty years, I have been captivated with Harriet "Mama Moses" Tubman and her fellow spirits of the Underground Railroad and what they can bestow upon the living. I have immersed myself in their conjures and traversed up and down the many historic trails and routes of freedom, meeting others who were dabbling in the mysticism of the U.G.R.R. or who were at least aware of it. I have shared rituals and ceremonies and written and lectured about the U.G.R.R. spirit world and their sacred gifts across North America. I have spent nights in their cemeteries, beside their graves—many unmarked without a headstone—communing, conjuring, and revering them.

The spirits of the freedom seekers have guided me through a doorway, back through the trails of freedom to gather their stories, their conjures, and their legacies. The very first Cairn and Cross I built as a symbol to honor the U.G.R.R. was upon grounds in St. Catharines with freedom seekers laying unmarked below. This combination of symbols is now the recognized grave marker among conjurers, workers, and even some official clergy and U.G.R.R. descendants for the forgotten spirits of the U.G.R.R. across North America, wherever and by whomever they are built. In this book, we will visit the mysteries of the Cairn and Cross as well as how to build and consecrate them and house those who visit thereafter from the realm of spirit.

I share all this because for validity it matters where I live and how I came to hear the voices of the U.G.R.R. and see their shadows cast by holy light. It matters because it's from here at the end of the U.G.R.R. that I learned the offerings, the magic, and where I first felt the uplifting blessings the spirits of freedom seekers can bestow to those who revere them well. Upon finishing this book, you will be armed with that formula and fully encouraged to enter their world and allow them to enter yours.

All of those years of practice resulting in much of the work within these pages and what it represents have not been without controversy. While I have been blessed to be befriended and gain trust among the descendants of freedom seekers and historic U.G.R.R. figures, there are also many Christians who feel they have a proprietary stake in the spiritual legacy of the Underground Railroad. Among them are those who feel disdain for my work, calling it "nefarious sorcery" and outright "devil worship."

For many in academic circles, I'm perceived as an outlaw, a renegade, a lowly witchdoctor—and a white one at that. This is because I shine a spotlight on the taboo shadow world of rootwork, voodoo, and conjure that runs on the tracks of the U.G.R.R.: something too often relegated to superstition, witchcraft, heresy, or even simple ghost stories. But this is hardly something I can control.

In order to immerse oneself and work with the spirit world of the U.G.R.R., all its realities must be comprehended. And when it comes to reality, many of the most notable figures of the U.G.R.R.—from Harriet Tubman, John Brown, Frederick Douglass, and Thomas Garret to Mary Ellen Pleasant and Sojourner Truth—were immersed in a spirituality encompassing everything from Christian mysticism and evangelical teachings to spiritualism and voodoo, and some of them drew from all of this at some point in their lives. This is not something that academic or historical societies have focused upon in the past, and, in fact, many have avoided it the best they can. And these histories do not even touch on how many of the freedom seekers and runaways themselves were conjurers, rootworkers, and adherents of various ATRs.

In order to draw from the U.G.R.R. spirit world, we have to know that it was all of these things, as well as acknowledging all its facets. Freedom fighting is a messy business, and it was no different for the U.G.R.R. When we work with the spirits of the U.G.R.R., we need them to know we understand their legacy; they need to know we honor all that they sacrificed for their freedom, including their families and their own lives. We need them to know we have gratitude in our hearts as we approach them, for their struggle and survival against slavery has made our world a better place. The spirits of the U.G.R.R. are true heroes worthy of veneration, and venerate them we shall.

This book is a grimoire, a guidebook, a formulary of spells and conjurations that pertain to Harriet "Mama Moses" Tubman and the spirits of the Underground Railroad. We will learn a good deal of necessary history, as much as a book of this nature can contain, but at the same time we will be learning the formula to invoke the spirits of those histories. We will explore many famous figures of the U.G.R.R. along with their conjurations. We will learn the Conjuration of Harriet "Mama Moses" Tubman, the General. We will come to know the Conjuration of John Brown, the Captain, as well as the Conjuration of Mary Ellen Pleasant, the Mistress.

We will also come to know the conjurations and invocation process of a host of spirit families, of which many members are nameless, forgotten souls who manifest and surround Mama Moses as her "Followers."

There are those who may find the material in my book to be challenging in regard to preconceived notions of rootwork as curses, domination spells, and fast luck, which have been influenced by the commercial and peddled popular brands of "southern conjure" and "hoodoo," much of it based upon fragments and reconstruction from a hyper-romanticized era in the early to mid 1900s I refer to as the "golden era." The truth of the matter is I believe much of the nuance of these traditions is being lost. In the 1940s, conjure and hoodoo in Dallas were very different from the voodoo of New Orleans and the gris-gris swamp magic surrounding it. From Louisiana across to Tampa, all the practices were vastly different, as was much of the lingo. From Jackson up through St. Louis to Chicago, across to Detroit, Cleveland, Buffalo, and on to New York City, all the traditions, formulas, and spellwork were different. Similarities existed, of course, but there was no one all-encompassing name to describe everything ranging from sorcery to faith healing, spiritual baptisms to juju, séance, or hoodoo. Nor was there an all-encompassing set of rules, traditions, or dogma. Also consider that entire regions from the Ozarks to the Appalachians were melting pots where traditions blended together and formed their own versions of conjure, different still from valley to mountain. What is being lost in my opinion is just how differently from one another the mystics of the early to mid 1900s performed their work.

For most there were no commercialized "condition oils," fancily dressed candles, or commercial powders. The true mystics had their own way of doing things, whether working with a specific spirit housed in a lonely boneyard around the bend or voicing their own incantations learned from no one and not shared with anyone other than the spirits they worked with. This is not to say that mysteries and formula were not passed down, but it wasn't in quite in the ways the modern commercialized and appropriated techniques purport. It's gotten to the point now where folks are using High John the Conqueror root without even knowing who he was and what he meant to the enslaved African, never mind how to invoke him or awaken his root's power. In fact, he is even being depicted on oil and candle labels as a white man or Spanish conquistador. In this book, we will learn about the true mystery of High John the Conqueror the folk hero, as well as his powerful magic and why it was sacred to the enslaved that were so brutally treated. Things like this happen because not enough actual practitioners of these traditions—the true mystics and renowned workers—passed enough of it on to others. There simply were not enough of these unique folks to go around; they were remote and mysterious at the best of times. Folks during this golden era would frequently travel across numerous state lines in order to seek out a powerful conjure doctor or root woman for their magic. And many of those old conjure doctors would first and foremost rely upon the "power of place" where they dwelled: the plants and herbs of their local climate and region, as well as the spiritual legacy of their own ancestors. Most of them had ancestors who had been enslaved, and terribly so. The mystical legacy that existed was less about fancy commercialized terms, powders, and oils and more about healing and heartfelt reverence for those that came before you, who might be buried just up the road or in your backyard. Ingredients for magic and healing might be picked from your own front yard.

Some of the processes in these pages will seem familiar to many, Christians, conjurers, and rootworkers alike. Some of the Christian mysticism may also put off the ardent neopagan, but that is a part of the U.G.R.R. and its spirit world. Truth be told, there has been no greater community of support than that of the neopagans and witches of North America. While I have traveled across the continent and presented at festivals and conferences with the Dragon Ritual Drummers, the Niagara Voodoo Shrine, or the New Orleans Voodoo Spiritual Temple, I found their thirst and desire for more information and formulas to work with Mama Moses and the spirits of the U.G.R.R. to be an inspiration and the impetus for providing this book of conjures. I have endeavored to share portions of a generation's worth of work and mysteries that I and a host of colleagues have unearthed, collected, created, and put into practice for those desiring to interact with, feed, and exalt inspiring and heroic spirits. No matter what our spiritual tradition, with an open heart and mind we can conjure, wield, and manifest via a spirit world uniquely North American and housed by spirits that are interconnected through a legacy of freedom and justice.

One point to remember is that there is no orthodoxy or dogma when it comes to conjure, rootwork, and voodoo. There is no single official set of rules, means, and ways. It all depends on where you live, the spiritual legacy and power of place it houses, and its connection to the African American experience. A unique aspect we will learn about in this book is that the U.G.R.R. indeed connected not only many parts of North America, but also its people and their ancestral history, and that goes for both black and white. The trails of freedom and their magic ran deep through the entire continent. The magical formula of spirit reverence that grows in my front yard here at the end of the U.G.R.R. grows too in yours; we are connected by arteries of ancestral blood and legacy so that we can all drink together from the cup of conjure and revere the spirit world that is the U.G.R.R.

The crucial focus of this book—and what truly matters—is the spirits of the U.G.R.R.: what they require, desire, and need. As we will see, they have been attainable and worked with for many generations in a smattering of ways across North America. However, this is the first time this information has been contained in one volume.

Conjuring Harriet "Mama Moses" Tubman

and the Spirits of the Underground Railroad

The Drinking Gourd

The Drinking Gourd
and North Star Doorway

Before we learn of their spirits and their magics, I want to share the first and simplest of conjures for the spirits of the U.G.R.R., to set the tone through the most basic of formulas: our prayers of intent.

The North Star was sung to and wished upon as the great navigator those on the U.G.R.R. looked to to guide them out of bondage and point the way north. To stand beneath and draw the light of the North Star down upon us is a central sacred work with the spirits of the U.G.R.R. The North Star is a mirror that still reflects back to us the very eyes of those who gazed up toward it in prayer, vow, panic, and, for some, eventual joy. For many who fled on the tracks of freedom this was the only aid they had. No other codes, mysteries, or promise of friends waiting farther on down the line was there for them to hold on to, just the hope that somehow it would all work out. The North Star was the encourager to keep going, the comforter from above, a devoted eye of the ancestors looking down upon their people with love.

This is the holiest celestial mystery definitive of the U.G.R.R. and its legacy: the North Star's ability to house and reflect back to us that which was conjured into it. Yes, the freedom seeker used it to navigate. It was a symbol and code among friends and supporters, immortalized as a holy light for those greatest achievements of self-emancipation ever known. But it was also a mirror, and a mirror retains all that it captures. For every victorious moment of a freedom seeker standing upon his or her metaphorical Land of Canaan, across the borderline of the "River Jordan" gazing upon her with unfathomable joy, there is sadness too. How does one find words to describe the level of sadness and tragedy retained and reflected back? We can look to the North Star with dry eyes and praise its heavenly light and all that it stood for, but all her mysteries must be grappled with. For she also captures forever the last moments of those who were not successful, whose tear-filled eyes gazed one last time at their comforter before their life was stolen away. Many of the old U.G.R.R. tracks to freedom are still in haunt; not all spirits who wander them have found their way into the arms of Mama Moses and her Followers or the shrines of their living descendants. Even today some of those that were successful now lie beneath parking lots, their names forgotten, headstones absent.

This is the nature of this tradition of conjure, why we do it, and the blessings exchanged between human and spirit: We help those who are still lost to navigate their way and continue to elevate the spirits of the U.G.R.R. by bringing them home to their families, whether they are here among the living or loves residing in the hereafter. For every spirit or mystery we work with and explore within this book, we strengthen our connection to the spirit world. For every Cairn and Cross we build, every mojo or talisman we create, every spiritual sung and invocation announced, we are enhancing our powers of conjuration toward this very work.

When you stand immersed in the North Star's subtle yet sacred light, let your focus blur to just beyond your peripheral so that the doorway that the mirror provides will open to you. Let your will and prayers center on the intent that the spirits continue to find their loved ones and friends that helped them and end in an embrace in spirit. Allow that aim be carried to the winds. Let every conjure you do for the spirits be unto this purpose, your shrine to the spirits of the U.G.R.R. act as a safe house, the symbols and the spirituals you sing and whisper a means of encouragement. Bring them to a place of comfort. And from there, for every time we work among the conjures of the U.G.R.R., let them finally embrace their loved ones, Mama Moses, the Diviners, and the Healers. Let them hear the call to séance and find solace among the spiritualists. Let them give the warrior handshake to Captain Brown. Once within the fold of the spirit world of the U.G.R.R., these spirits will be able to choose their trail from there: to carry on to their god and the angels, to arrive and love their descendants, or to live among the active spirits so that the work can continue.

Every hug and handshake shared in the spirit world of the U.G.R.R. is possible because of the sacred work that still must be done. We must still fill the spirit world with light, protection, and sustenance and never forget its need to exist. For we will always need this spirit world and its heroic fraternity where white and black fought together, whose bonds have remained intact into the afterlife. It's up to us to add to that afterlife and nurture it, making it stronger and safer and sharing it with those who possess a capacity to take the flame and illuminate their part of the continual interconnected quilt of freedom. Now more than ever we need to be able to draw from this beautiful spirit world, conjure it into our reality, and in doing so feed and strengthen it.

Many spirits have already chosen to work among the ghost tracks, trails, homesteads, statuary, altars, and graves of prominence so that those who were forgotten can continue their journey and reach eternal freedom. And for each of us working under the North Star exalting and feeding those working spirits, we enable and uplift them hand in hand.

Find Your Connection with the North Star Mirror

No matter where we live—in light-saturated cities or under clear country skies—the North Star is visible up above, twinkling in the heavens.

Locate the North Star, also known as the polestar, wherever you are. You can do this by finding the secret coded companion she sits beside: the Drinking Gourd, named so by the Africans for its similarity to a literal hollow gourd used for drinking, immortalized in spirituals but most commonly known as the Big Dipper, and to us in this tradition as the Cup of Conjure. City dwellers may have to travel a few blocks to get to a good place to view it, but many of the practices in these pages require a little bit of work at times to achieve, even what appears to be the most basic.

The Big Dipper is a constellation that never sets in the northern sky. It circles around the North Star. Use whatever means you have to find the cardinal direction north in your area, then look for the stars that form a bowl on the end of a handle. Folks name constellations for what they look like, and this grouping looks like a dipper or a drinking gourd. Now look at the bowl of the Big Dipper. The two stars that make up the end of the cupping shape form a line, and if you follow the line out of the Big Dipper and off into space with your eyes, you will find the bright beacon of the North Star.

Once you've located the Big Dipper, take some time to make a connection. Ponder the Drinking Gourd, its mysteries and cloaked meaning, and how many drank from that very cup to achieve eventual freedom. Then connect the two celestial mysteries: Once you have drawn the line to the North Star, fixate upon it, gazing and bonding with it by any means you can. Remember, it is a mirror, the gateway to the U.G.R.R. spirit world that will swing open. At this moment you are the gatekeeper.

Let your vision blur just a bit, at least to your peripheral, and you will not only be the gatekeeper but a beacon. You will be a lantern bearer, your spirit will become illuminated by its holy light, and the spirits will see you—through the buildings that may be around you and the noise that may surround you, they will hear you.

Imagine at this moment that the wandering spirits that were lost on the trails of freedom will catch a glimpse of you, that those who are already elevated and exist among the U.G.R.R. spirit world will spot your light, and indeed Mama Moses will see you too. Mama Moses and her Followers will look into your soul and know it as kind, as an ancestor or as a friend. Who knows how many other conjurers on any given night are gazing upon the North Star's mirror for this simplest, yet sacred act and how many more spirits still wander, eyes fixed upon her light?

Speak aloud or just in a whisper, and let the spirits know you are a lantern bearer and that your shrines and work are for them. Each of us engaging in this practice creates our own grid in an ever-evolving constellation of illuminated souls fixed upon the earth. We are the beacons, the "shooflys" in the old code for the trusted allies on the Underground Railroad, the guides.

The Lantern Bearer's Prayer

Do this work as often as possible or when time presents itself. Praying to the North Star will enhance your connection to Mama Moses and the spirits of the U.G.R.R. Reciting the prayer out loud is the most effective.

To the Drinking Gourd high in the sky,

Let me drink from your chalice of silvery light;

Let me open the gate whilst quenched from your holy cup of conjure.

Sweet North Star, great lantern bearer of the sky,

Mirror who reflects God's light from afar,

Let my lantern bear your sacred light

and I will cast it to the shadows.

Let those who still have rivers to cross be guided by my lantern's light.

Let a column of your holy light beam down upon my home.

Let our lanterns shine, connected, eternal and forevermore.

Young Harriet Tubman

The Conjuration of Harriet "Mama Moses" Tubman

I was the conductor of the Underground Railroad for eight years, and
I can say what most conductors can't say—I never ran my train off the
track and I never lost a passenger.

—HARRIET TUBMAN

In the spirit world of the U.G.R.R. Harriet Tubman is the "General"—
and for good reason. It was a title bestowed upon her in a mystical and
spiritual proclamation by none other than the martyr, the insurrectionist,
and her friend and brother-in-arms "Captain" John Brown. She was fond
of this name till her dying days. Harriet Tubman was a mystic, a healer, a
warrior—she was Mama Moses who, like her biblical namesake, led her
people to freedom.

Before we begin to work with the powerful and beautiful spirit of
Mama Moses, let's have a look at some of the highlights of this fascinat-
ing holy woman's life.

Harriet Tubman's Early Years

Harriet Tubman was born Araminta Ross in approximately 1822 in
Dorchester County, Maryland. Until she reached young adulthood, she

was called Minty. Her mother, whose name was Rit, was a slave with a position in the "big house" where the plantation master lived and was a conjure woman like her mother had been before her: Minty's grandmother, presumably renamed Modesty by her slaveholders, was an Ashanti who had been brought over from what is now Ghana. Minty was always aware of her Ashanti ancestry. Minty's father, Ben Ross, who was born into slavery in America but had his freedom granted to him in middle age, was a skilled woodsman and woodworker, a man respected by everyone: his fellow enslaved, free people of color, and the masters for whom he labored.

During the time she was enslaved, Minty was beaten brutally. By the time she was six years old, Minty was already caring for her baby brother, so she was then sent out to labor as a nursemaid and to provide child care in other homesteads. There young Minty suffered more physical abuse. She learned to improvise quickly and to wear numerous layers of clothing to absorb the constant whippings and beatings.

> I grew up like a neglected weed, – ignorant of liberty, having no experience of it. Then I was not happy or contented.
>
> —HARRIET TUBMAN IN BENJAMIN DREW, *THE REFUGEES*

Her young life would change forever after a brutal and fateful assault by a wicked man. At about the age of fifteen, while running into town for goods, she encountered a fellow enslaved youth she knew personally who had slipped away from his plantation without permission. His furious overseer soon appeared and wanted Minty to help apprehend the boy. She refused, and when the boy ran for it, the overseer threw a several-pound metal weight toward him. It struck Minty in the head instead. This was a severe and life-threatening injury. Bloodied and experiencing head trauma, she spent days drifting in and out of consciousness. Her master did not think she was worth medical attention and had her back at hard labor within weeks.

This head injury is considered the catalyst that brought on her life-long visions, prophetic dreams, and hearing the voice of God. It was her initiation into the world of the mysteries. Spirituality had been a part of her core from a young age; from Bible stories told to her to the lore and legends of her maternal grandmother from Ghana, young Minty was aware of the worlds of African spirits as well as the Holy Spirit and everything in between. One of the foremost Tubman historians, Dr. Kate Clifford Larsen, says in *Bound for the Promised Land*, "Tubman's religiosity was a deeply personal spiritual experience, unquestionably rooted in powerful evangelical teachings, but also reinforced and nurtured through strong African cultural traditions." Her history of spirituality and the head injury came together to form a perfect storm to create the mystic she would become and the general in the war she would soon fight. These would be the foundations of a holy woman, rootworker, healer, and warrior. Young Minty had also seen firsthand that resistance was viable, even if it might seem futile at times. She not only knew all about Nat Turner's initially powerful rebellion and the brutal result from 1831, but considered him a local hero, as many of the enslaved did.

Her family's slave master Edward Brodess had already sold some of Minty's siblings south, never to be heard from again. Not long after her injury, he made it known that he planned on selling her youngest brother, a child named Moses. Rit hid her infant son for over a month with the help of fellow slaves, as well as some free people of color. When the time finally came that Brodess and the buyer were to enter Rit's dwelling to retrieve the child, Rit resisted and threw a curse at them, promising death to whomever touched her child. The sale was called off. This act of resistance had an impact upon Minty in more ways than one.

> God's time [Emancipation] is always near. He set the North Star
> in the heavens; He gave me the strength in my limbs;
> He meant I should be free.
>
> —HARRIET TUBMAN TO EDNAH DOW CHENEY, IN KATE CLIFFORD LARSEN,
> BOUND FOR THE PROMISED LAND

Through years of child care and nursemaid duties Minty had gained a reputation for doing extremely hard labor, preferably alone—which was not uncommon for enslaved women—in order to avoid brutal treatment from the house mistress and sexual advances by the masters. During these years of hard labor, a new opportunity sealed her future as an Underground Railroad conductor and warrior. Minty's master allowed her to hire herself out: for an annual fee paid to her master she could work for herself, enabling her to buy her own livestock and grow her own food to sell and trade in the hopes of saving enough money to possibly purchase her own freedom. This era brought her back into close proximity with her father, Ben Ross, which made Minty very happy.

Being in close quarters to her father brought her more indispensable tools. While surrounded by mostly black men working on docks and in timber crews, Tubman was able to learn secret codes of communication and networks of travel that were mysteries among black mariners. The mariners were familiar with a world seemingly far away, including the shipyards and ports in Baltimore, communities and landscapes all along the Chesapeake Bay, right up to New Jersey and Pennsylvania. The black mariners and Tubman's father were able to share safe locations as well as ones fraught with danger. This secret language that was essentially a map and code of communication would come in handy soon enough.

As a young woman living through harsh realities that enslavement brought, blessed and a young prophetess as she may be, she still felt the very human desire for love. Her first love was for a man named John Tubman, a free man of color. Relationships between slaves and free people of color were not uncommon at that time or in that region, although they brought with them a lot of complications. Any children born to such a couple were considered property of the slave master of the mother. Their time together is shrouded in mystery, but John and Minty were married in 1844 when they "jumped the broom." They lived together in a small cottage, were for a time a happy and loving couple, and it was then that she changed her name from Minty to "Harriet" in what is believed to be a combination of a religious conversion and the honoring of a relative, quite possibly her mother. She would be known as Harriet Tubman from then on.

Harriet experienced a bout of ill health in 1849, during which she had potent nightmares of being sold south. Harriet came to find out that her master was indeed actively trying to unload her because of her sickness—regardless of her marriage. Between her impending sale and the continual enslavement of her relatives, she began to pray fervently that her master would change his mind. She later said, "I prayed all night long for my master till the first of March; and all the time he was bringing people to look at me, and trying to sell me." Once a sale appeared final, she said, "I changed my prayer. First of March I began to pray, 'Oh Lord, if you ain't never going to change that man's heart, kill him, Lord, and take him out of the way'" (Bradford, *Harriet Tubman: The Moses of Her People*). A week later her master Edward Brodess was dead as the result of an unknown illness.

But this was not the end of Harriet's trouble. His estate would soon be distributed, and there was now a serious chance that Harriet would be sold off and her family split up. This was not an option for her: it was now or never. Her desire to escape slavery became more than just a yearning for justice and started to take shape as a plan. This would be when her visions, voices, and blessings must be acted upon: she would be free or die trying.

I had reasoned this out in my mind; there was one of two things I had a right to, liberty, or death; if I could not have one, I would have the other; for no man should take me alive; I should fight for my liberty as long as my strength lasted, and when the time came for me to go, the Lord would let them take me.

—HARRIET TUBMAN IN SARAH BRADFORD,
HARRIET TUBMAN: THE MOSES OF HER PEOPLE, 1886

Harriet tried to convince John to flee with her and members of her family heading north to freedom. He, however, by all accounts was not interested. He was a free man, after all, had a business, and, despite his wife's pleas, wanted none of it. It was no different on the night she fled. She got word to her mother that she was leaving, and that night she sang a coded spiritual to her fellow trusted slaves: "I will meet you in the morning, when I reach the promised land, on the other side of Jordon for I am bound for the Promised Land" (Bradford, *Harriet Tubman: The Moses of Her People*). To this day her exact route and where she took refuge along the way are debated, but it is known she fled in the middle of the night for a journey of nearly ninety miles (145 kilometers). Following the North Star through Delaware and up to Pennsylvania, her path would have taken her anywhere from one to three weeks on foot. This had to have been a monumental initiation for her will and spirit: to leave the family she loved so much behind, to abandon her home and husband. Those hungry weeks must have seemed an eternity.

She never revealed any details about her first trip, but certainly did share her thoughts on the moment she realized she was free: "When I found I had crossed that line, I looked at my hands to see if I was the same person. There was such a glory over everything; the sun came like gold through the trees, and over the fields, and I felt like I was in Heaven" (Bradford, *Harriet Tubman: The Moses of Her People*). This is the moment when the legend of Harriet Tubman would take root. Tasting freedom, she would become the mysterious and soon to be "wanted dead or alive" conductor, a spirit in the night, leading as many others to it as she could. Her haunting and feared persona was just emerging.

The Legend Grows

*I was a stranger in a strange land. My father, my mother, my brothers,
and sisters, and friends were in Maryland.*

—Harriet Tubman in Sarah Bradford,
Harriet Tubman: The "Moses of Her People"

Harriet Tubman's first return trip back into hostile territory from the
Free North was to retrieve members of her family, and in fact many of
her sojourns back and forth were to gather family, friends, and colleagues.
In 1850 the U.S. Congress passed the Fugitive Slave Act, making the
penalties for aiding escaped slaves very severe, and even in free states law
enforcement had to help capture and return escapees to their "owners."
The free states could no longer be an option for resettling refugees from
slavery for Tubman.

*I wouldn't trust Uncle Sam with my people no longer,
I brought 'em all clear off to Canada.*

—Harriet Tubman in Sarah Bradford,
Harriet Tubman: The "Moses of Her People"

Her new base of operations was now in St. Catharines, Ontario, in the
Niagara Region of Canada. It was just far enough from the U.S. border
to make it hard for bounty hunters to enter town and escape with their
lives intact. It offered a community that to a degree supported the freedom
seekers, and a section of town that still stands today became their Promised Land of "Canaan." Her house of prayer and base of operations was
the historic British Methodist Episcopal (BME) Church, Salem Chapel,
a still-functioning congregation and celebrated place in Canadian history—served and operated by freedom seeker descendants.

Abolitionist and spiritualist William Lloyd Garrison was the first to
call Tubman "Moses," in reference to the prophet in the Book of Exodus

who led the Hebrews out of bondage to the pharaoh. Incidentally, Tubman took much of her biblical inspiration from the Old Testament with its focus on deliverance and was not fond of the narrative contained in the New Testament, feeling it promoted obedience among the enslaved.

During these years of conducting freedom seekers to safety Tubman's legend grew and her mysticism gained repute not only among those who knew her well, but also those who traveled with her, aided her, and even those endeavoring to catch her, for at this point there was a sizable reward for the capture of Harriet "Mama Moses" Tubman. Her seemingly supernatural powers, psychic visions, incantations, and unique cures were the stuff of a conjure woman—it was and is a part of her identity to this day, at least for those who care to shed light upon it.

Harriet's friend and colleague, the legendary abolitionist Thomas Garrett, wrote of her mystical side (collected in James McGowan, *Station Master on the Underground Railroad*), "I inform you that Harriet has a good deal of the Quaker about her. She is a firm believer of spiritual manifestations." Garrett, himself a spiritualist, knew that she possessed extrasensory powers and abilities. In his writings he relays how many times she seemed to know when he had money for her, "whether clairvoyance, or the divine impression on her mind from the source of all power, I cannot tell; but, certain it was that she had a guide within herself other than the written word." Garrett also said of her, "I never met any person of any color who had more confidence in the voice of God." Tubman spent a great deal of time with Garrett and was present at some of his spiritualist meetings, contributing to and honing work with spirits and ancestors and communing with the "divine."

Runaways interviewed by William Wells Brown in St. Catharines, and quoted in *Station Master on the Underground Railroad*, said, "She had supernatural powers and the 'charm'" ... "The women herself felt she had the charm, and this feeling, no doubt, nerved her up, gave her courage, and made all who followed her feel safe in her hands." She was known to wander various cemeteries in solitude in the "witching hours" when time presented itself.

New England author, journalist, and philanthropist Franklin Benjamin Sanborn is also quoted in Station Master on the Underground Railroad as saying, "She is the most shrewd and practical person in the world yet she is a firm believer in omens, dreams and warnings . . . Her dreams, misgivings and forewarnings ought not to be omitted in any life of hers, particularly when it comes to John Brown." And we won't. When it came to the larger-than-life insurrectionist and feared freedom fighter "Captain" John Brown, there was indeed a cosmic and spiritual connection between them, as we will explore in a later chapter. Suffice it to say here that it was Brown who bestowed upon her a title that lasts till this day as her legacy, that of "General Tubman," when he was in St. Catharines seeking her counsel before the raid on Harpers Ferry. He said to her that when he needed to feel her presence and inspiration he would call out loud three times "General Tubman" as an invocation. It was a mystical proclamation to honor her immense work of freeing slaves, knowledge of the land, and unrivaled spiritual force. They were warriors. Unlike their mutual friend Frederick Douglass, Tubman was all in for the captain's plans for Harpers Ferry; she was all in when it came to his brand of justice and dolling out death to slavers and the like; she was all in when it came to fighting slavery by any means necessary. She would sadly never see him again; he was hanged for his raid on Harpers Ferry. Tubman mourned Brown as a martyr.

Harriet Tubman was celebrated, supported, and an inspiration to many of the heavy hitters paramount to the U.G.R.R. Frederick Douglass, who himself escaped slavery and was the most famous of abolitionists and orators for the cause; William Still, the Philadelphia-based black abolitionist and impeccable recordkeeper; and William Lloyd Garrison, a prominent white abolitionist, were all interconnected, corresponded with each other, and were soldiers on the front lines of funneling freedom seekers to safe haven. Tubman had love for them all, but drew huge amounts of inspiration from the amazing Douglass. In the hard years of Tubman's life spent in midnight swamps, in hills, and in disguise, Douglass knew how hard she tried and toiled in constant danger and always had high regard for her, something that brought her much comfort.

She continued to be almost a ghostlike entity to those in the slave states, who feared her and her supernatural ways. She was known to come out of some of her trances and dreams with knowledge of an ambush that lay in wait and change course. And they would come to find out later that there had indeed been an ambush waiting. She wielded her "charm" and spiritual powers as the most feared conductor of the U.G.R.R., divining by animal activity, clouds, rocks, and bones as well as her dreams and visions. She reputedly carried a gourd as a container, housing roots and herbs that she would shake in certain times of need. She was known to say on certain trips that those in tow should pray to their god and she would pray to hers and things will be just fine.

From Canada to New York, Maryland to Massachusetts, and Pennsylvania to Virginia, she haunted the trails of freedom, gathering and guiding hundreds of freedom seekers in her time. Her legacy and lore spread from plantation to plantation among the enslaved and those who endeavored to flee; tales of renowned tactics of trickery and cunning reigned. As far away as Texas, those in bondage knew of Mama Moses. A solitary runaway from Texas is noted in *Lay My Burden Down: A Folk History of Slavery* (ed. B. A. Botkin) as saying, "I's hoping and praying all the time I meet up with that Harriet Tubman woman who takes slaves to Canada. She always travels the underground railroad, as they calls it, travels by night and hides out in the day. She sure sneaks them out of the south, and I think shes the brave woman." She threw tricks and outsmarted bounty hunters; she was known to pick up roosters and carry them to pretend to be a slave while in hostile territory as well as pretending to read when necessary, for the word was out that she could not. Like Moses himself she conjured and defied the odds.

She carried a revolver in those years and wasn't afraid to use it, whether on slavers, bounty hunters, or the hounds they enlisted. Her "piece" was also reputedly an extra incentive for wavering travelers on her track. Once a journey had begun, it was too dangerous for runaways to change their mind and return to the plantation; they would surely be tortured or bribed to give up valuable information. So in those weak moments she was known to pull out her gun and say, "Dead people tell no tales. You go on or die, one way or another you'll be free," according to Earl Conrad in *Harriet Tubman*.

The Civil War and After

Harriet Tubman's time on the Railroad would come to an end when the American Civil War began, but her legacy as a conjure woman and warrior was far from over.

God won't let master Lincoln beat the South till he does the right thing.
—HARRIET TUBMAN IN JAMES MCGOWAN AND WILLIAM KASHATUS,
HARRIET TUBMAN: A BIOGRAPHY

When the Civil War broke out in 1861, Tubman was frustrated with the fact that slavery was still legal in the southern states and felt it was futile to fight toward victory till all were emancipated. She nevertheless supported the Union, left Canada, and actively sought a place within their ranks to help. She soon became a renowned nurse, and offered valuable intelligence on the trails and routes she had been successfully navigating in her years as a clandestine U.G.R.R. conductor.

As a nurse, her cures in dentistry and for smallpox, along with her seeming immunity to the diseases, also reinforced her reputation as a blessed mystic. Her folk medicine combined spirituals and incantations that had been honed on the freedom trails. Her presence was celebrated among the black Union soldiers. As quoted in *Station Master on the Underground*

Railroad, it was said, "When the Negro put on the Blue (joined Union Army), Moses was in her glory and traveled from camp to camp, being always treated in the most respectful manner . . . These black men would have died for this woman, for they believed she had the 'charm.'"

In 1863 Lincoln issued the Emancipation Proclamation, making the war something Tubman could now really get behind and support on a tactical level—and in one instance in a way that is legend. Her knowledge of the lands and covert activity on the U.G.R.R. as well as her warrior spirit would be paramount to the success of the famous Combahee River Raid. Tubman had already contributed intel-wise in the capture of Jacksonville, Florida, but with the Combahee raid she became the first woman to lead an armed assault during the Civil War. In June of 1863 Tubman led three steamboats, maneuvering through Confederate mines, to land and raid several plantations. Once ashore the Union army set flame to plantations, raided supplies, and destroyed infrastructure. They also freed up to 750 slaves. Steamboat whistles rang out to signal to the enslaved to escape and board the vessels. The chaos was intense; men, women, and children were clamoring to get on the boats with livestock, food, and supplies. "I never saw such a sight," Tubman said (Clinton, *Harriet Tubman: The Road to Freedom*). Almost all of the newly freed men immediately joined the Union army. Harriet Tubman was a general, indeed.

Tubman would also later work with Colonel Robert Gould Shaw at the battle of Fort Wagner, where she made and served his last meal. In *Bound for the Promised Land*, she said of the terrible fighting, "And then we saw the lightning, and that was the guns; and then we heard the thunder, and that was the big guns; and then we heard the rain falling, and that was the drops of blood falling; and when we came to get the crops, it was dead men that we reaped."

For the last two years of the Civil War Tubman tended to Union soldiers as a nurse, continued to help free slaves in raids, and inspired

Harriet Tubman, 1911

soldiers both black and white. It would not be till 1899 that she received a military pension and commendation for her work in the war, however.

Mama Moses would marry again in 1869. Her second love was a Civil War veteran and black man named Nelson Davis, who was about twenty-two years her junior, and they were together for twenty love-filled years.

Her later years were spent in Auburn, New York, tending to her now completely free family—those that she could find. Along with her mother and father, much of her extended family lived together in her home and boardinghouse. She spent those years also supporting the women's suffrage movement alongside Susan B. Anthony, as well as hosting biographers and media and sharing her stories and legacy. But times were always tough financially. In 1897 she was happy to be acknowledged by Britain's Queen Victoria for her unique humanitarian legacy and contribution to fighting slavery. The queen awarded her a silver medal, a letter of accommodation, money, and a white silk shawl that she proudly wore in her twilight years.

Harriet "Mama Moses" Tubman succumbed to pneumonia on March 10, 1913, surrounded by friends and family. Shortly before her death, her final words, as quoted in the *Auburn Citizen* on March 11, were, "I go to prepare a place for you." Mama Moses was buried with semi-military honors at Fort Hill Cemetery in Auburn, and her grave is a place of pilgrimage and a veritable shrine.

We see a woman in Mama Moses who was undoubtedly a mystic in the truest sense. This woman faced racism in its rawest form born into the subhuman treatment of slavery but still found a way through her spirituality and courage to fight for freedom. This woman fought to preserve her family and demonstrated her devotion to kin by risking her very life on numerous occasions so they too could be free. This woman suffered the most horrendous racial injustices at the hands of white men and women yet possessed the complex capacity to later accept them as friends, confidants, and spiritual colleagues. We see a woman in Mama Moses who fought like a warrior in a way to make men of her time envious and whose cunning was invaluable to trained military tacticians. She was a master at the arts of disguise and distraction, avoiding being captured in the hostile territories she returned to time and again. We see a healer, and a mysterious one at that, with cures and means drawing from the esoteric as well as pragmatic. We see a woman in Mama Moses who fought for justice on every level till her dying days, bringing equality to men and women of every creed and color. We have a spirit in Mama Moses that is tangible and attainable for council, blessings, and inspiration as we endeavor and fight for our own freedom, humanity, and spiritual needs. The spirit of Harriet "Mama Moses" Tubman is still holding court, and she still has many gifts to give for those with many rivers still to cross.

The Elevation of Mama Moses

While this book is a first as a grimoire of work pertaining to the Underground Railroad spirit world as a whole, and while I have dedicated over seventeen years of work and conjuration to Mama Moses, when it comes to reverence for Harriet Tubman I am far from the first. That she was buried with semi-military honors, presided over by local, state, and federal government officials, is an honor few receive. This is a type of ceremony that immortalizes a person and elevates her to a place of reverence. Her grave almost immediately became a place of pilgrimage for descendants and surviving freedom seekers, clergy of many faiths and adherents to numerous religious practices that came to honor her, as well as average people inspired to pay their respects. All of these acts, prayers, and exaltation make a spirit that much more tangible and accessible in a way that is not common. This is an honor, and her spirit accepted the charge.

Within years of her passing many folks claimed to have been visited by the spirit of Harriet Tubman, whether in dreams, visions, or séance and divination. Her spirit had even manifested in our physical realm to the point of being called a ghost or "haint" at some of the famous locations where she walked, lived, fought, loved, and prayed. Within a very short time her spirit was already manifesting, traveling and arriving where she was called to go whether of her own volition or via the petition of others.

In those short years after her death, in fact, many of the deceased historic figures of the U.G.R.R. continued to manifest among us. Many of them too had received elaborate ceremonial burials and reverence for their martyrdom, and properties, statuary, and plaques marked their places of renowned valor and humanitarian work. These few unique spirits, who while living had changed the fabric of society in a just and clandestine network, were still compelled to be connected in spirit. They forged bonds that lasted past a lifetime, and that is really such a rare, sacred, and beautiful thing to behold. Slowly but surely these spirits began to gather and continue to be connected in tangible ways.

In the era before and after WWII, in the midst of the Great Migration circa 1910–1970 when millions of southern black Americans traveled north to the industrial cities, hoodoo, voodoo, and conjure also proliferated. Some of the mystics and conjurers from both Canada and the United States were claiming to be able to work with the spirit of Harriet Tubman, known as Black Moses and Auntie Freedom. In the late 1960s and early '70s Harriet Tubman prayer cards circulated in Detroit, Michigan, a city that was a gateway of freedom during the U.G.R.R.—named "Midnight" in U.G.R.R. code—leading to Windsor, Ontario, across the Detroit River. In 1978 Harriet Tubman was commemorated on a U.S. postal stamp still in circulation to this day. In 1979 renowned American artist Paul Collins released his famous painting *The Underground Railroad* featuring Harriet Tubman and freedom seekers traversing a nighttime swamp. This painting sold and still sells prints in the hundreds of thousands. It immediately adorned churches, spiritualist temples, government buildings, museums, and homes.

By the 1990s there were adherents to Santeria, aka Regla Lucumi, in New York City who had welcomed Harriet Tubman as an Egun, the elevated ancestors within this tradition, as well as vodou adherents welcoming her into a family of Ogou, a nation of spirits within Haitian vodou. In the 1990s, Tubman's legacy and spirit were publicized to unprecedented levels by the sacred poetry and reverence of Brooklyn's Linda Cousins-Newton. And in June 2000, Harriet "Mama Moses" Tubman was honored by Ghana's first female chief, Nana Osei Boakye, who oversaw the "enstooling" of Mama Moses as the first known ancestor to be posthumously acknowledged as a "Queen Mother," naming her "Nana Awo Boatema II," which was also made possible in part by the incredible work and devotion of Cousins-Newton.

In 2011 I cofacilitated a ceremonial honoring with Prince Bamidele Bajowa of the royal house of Rebuja in Nigeria to bestow blessings and a title upon Mama Moses, as well as a sacrament offered for her followers who were of Yoruba descent. In 2014 the asteroid 241528 Tubman was named for her by the IAU Minor Planet Center. Statuary of Mama Moses adorns many cities in North America where she once walked, and in 2016 the U.S. Treasury Department announced that Harriet Tubman would appear on the forthcoming redesign of the U.S. twenty dollar bill. And on March 11, 2017, the Harriet Tubman Underground Railroad National Historical Park in Maryland opened to the public.

These are but a few instances demonstrating her exalted legacy. The spirit of Harriet Tubman was elevated and chose to join the ranks of glorified ancestors to humanity long ago. She continues to bless, guide, and manifest among those who call to her sacred spirit. A statue of "Nana" Tubman now stands in Aburi, Ghana, her ancestral home and birthplace of her maternal grandmother, Modesty.

Working with Harriet "Mama Moses" Tubman

As we can see from these highlights of her incredible blessed life and unique skill sets, there are numerous reasons that everyone from rootworkers, witches, and pagans to members of the African traditional religions and Christian conjurers would revere Mama Moses and want to petition for her blessings. She helps those seeking knowledge of cures and folk medicines, where at times she will inspire and plant within you a previously unknown conjure or cure as well as the rhyme and reason behind a particular magic you seek to create. She can be called on to help remove binds or blocks holding us back: abusive relationships, addictions, or other things that hinder our growth and freedom. She can aid us in opening chains and shackles of our own design: habits and emotions that do not serve us well and attitudes within us that need to be changed in order for us to truly grow past our usual ways and means. She can be petitioned to help us find our path toward that which we seek: new jobs and careers as well as creative projects that may seem unattainable or finishing off spiritual work seemingly stagnant and unrealized. She assists folks in finding their ancestral roots and brings them to the well of their descendants—especially people of African descent. She is, after all, an African Queen Mother, a Nana whose stool sits with her royal ancestral contemporaries in Ghana. She can guide us though dark times in our life, reminding us to persevere and that there is no mountain that can't be climbed, no river we cannot cross. She and her followers can illuminate with their spectral lanterns otherwise dark paths we would have trouble navigating and traversing, whether those routes are physical or esoteric. Mama Moses and her followers can be called to for "faith healing" as she and her Healers can be invoked to lay their spirit hands upon you or your loved ones and lend their strength in the healing that you seek. As well Mama Moses and her Followers can help enhance and hone our divination and seership. The reasons to seek her blessings are truly countless, to be honest, but there is one thing Mama Moses is never called for—and that is to harm or curse.

Mama Moses and her holy spirit, blessed by her god and ancestors, and draped in divine glory, is not to be called on to hurt a single person or aid in any magic that would. There are plenty of spiritual entities for that sort of thing, but she is not one of them, and neither are her Followers. Now if one is in an abusive or unhealthy relationship, for example—and this is a conjure blessing I have seen her deliver on for many folks over the years, almost all of them women—one still needs to focus on the task at hand: being free of it. It's always best in such circumstances to center your intent on release from the relationship and attaining what you need to leave and claim your soul, your life, and your freedom. This is a powerful blessing she does indeed bestow rather than calling down retribution. And of course one would call to her for the simple blessing of her just manifesting and gifting but a drop of her spiritual power that can change you on an alchemical level.

So as we can see, we can all call to Mama Moses for blessings from which, if asked for and petitioned correctly and from the right angle, pure intention can be realized. The spiritual and ancestral well of Mama Moses is an inspiring and powerful concoction and can truly change us and our surroundings for the absolute better.

The Altar for Mama Moses

Let's break down how to set up an altar or workspace for Mama Moses with her offerings and ways to connect and commune with her sacred spiritual force. It is most beneficial in many spiritual traditions—as a basic premise—to create an altar or shrine to not only honor but also please the intended spiritual entity. This is a place to commune and work with the spirit whether at home or out in nature, a portal to their realm. Not everyone can build a large shrine to Mama Moses with all of her tools and items, but small altars can still be quite effective.

CLEANSING YOUR SPACE

It is standard practice to cleanse your space before you set up your altar. Making the space sacred will change the energy of it so that when you place your items there, it will be ready for a spirit's presence. It's good to enlist Florida Water or Hoyt's Cologne, both commonly used colognes with a high alcohol content and strong aromatic quintessence, by sprinkling the surface and area with one. Holy water sprinkled or incense wafted about the area is also a good practice to do just before building a shrine to Mama Moses. Better yet, enlist more than one of the aforementioned. Burning incense will also remove any residual energetic charge in the area you want to dedicate to her—or any shrine for that matter.

It is worth noting that Hoyt's Cologne is the traditional means used most by North American hoodoo and conjure workers, commonly found in certain barbershops and salons, especially during the "golden era" I have previously referred to. Florida Water comes from the more Caribbean-influenced communities and cultures. With the proliferation of ATRs and those that appropriate them, Florida Water has become the far more popular concoction in this modern era.

ALTAR SPACES

Your altar, shrine, or workspace to honor Mama Moses can be any surface or place that you have available—even a shelf will do. The shrine is akin to an ancestor altar, a place that houses items that the intended spirit was fond of and would bring them comfort and familiarity when they are present. You can use fabric to cover the surface or not; it's up to you and the creativity you are inspired to. There are shrines to Mama Moses that are small wooden shelves with some of her tools and larger ones that have all the accoutrements we will list here for her as well as skulls and skeletal decorations to represent the dead. There are folks that house her in a pot or cauldron similar to the way of working with the Caribbean spirit La Madama. Then there are folks like me with an entire house dedicated to her with shrines to Mama Moses and her Followers throughout. It's really up to you, and it will undoubtedly change as time and the manifestation of spirits grow.

Your shrine, whatever form it takes, is a space that is dedicated to Mama Moses and her Followers. It is a place where you can go to focus on her blessings and spirit and a nexus that will be a portal to the inspiring world of her and the spirits of the U.G.R.R. The shrine to Mama Moses is a location where you can give her prayers and offerings and you can ask blessings of her and seek her favor for your needs. At the very least, for starters, a photo of Mama Moses, a glass of water, a candle, and the conjure symbol will be enough to get your space in a position to honor and please her.

ACCOUTREMENTS FOR MAMA MOSES

The items and tools listed below can be used to create an altar or workspace to commune with and revere Mama Moses and can be left as-is or added to as your shrine grows. As time and familiarity bring you into your work, don't question whatever presents itself or speaks to you as a tool, item, or image for her altar: that is spirit talking.

- A photo of Harriet Tubman. There are a few wonderful ones out there, but the photos in this book are my favorites.

- A glass of water. This is paramount for most spiritual traditions that honor the glorious dead. Water is life and can quench a spirit's thirst.

- A candle. Preferably use a jar or seven-day candle; they are the safest and last the longest for a shrine and altar. There is no wrong color of candle for her, but white candles are my favorite for working with Mama Moses.

- The conjure symbol for the spirits of the U.G.R.R. This can be on paper, in a frame, or drawn out on a surface within the shrine.

- A Bible. Mama Moses was immersed in Christianity. Whether you consider her Evangelical, Methodist, or Presbyterian, she was devout and drew inspiration in particular from the Old Testament.

- A Christian cross. Again, Christianity was foundational to her spirituality; it is something that will please her spirit and show you understand and respect her devotion.

- African carvings, statues, or masks of Ghanaian and Ashanti origin if possible. Nana Tubman also practiced African cultural traditions and is a Queen Mother.

- An image of the "Freedom Seeker." This can be on paper, in a frame, or drawn out on a surface within the shrine.

- Earth or rocks/pebbles from any of the many locations, statues, and plaques connected to the U.G.R.R. across North America.

- A gourd. She was reputed to carry a gourd-like pouch that contained roots, herbs, and other curios or "charms." Any dried hollow gourd would be good, potentially filled with herbs, roots, and whatever else may speak to you as you work with her.

- A small jar of river, swamp, lake, or marsh waters that were part of the U.G.R.R.

- High John, Dixie John, or Chewin' John root. (We'll learn more about these plants in the chapter on High John the Conqueror.)

- Healing, medicinal, or magical herbs. These could be bay leaves, wormwood, or devil's shoestring.

- Railway spikes

- Photos of any of her U.G.R.R. colleagues and fellow warriors. Some examples would be John Brown, Frederick Douglass, Sojourner Truth, Thomas Garrett, and William Still.

- A lantern. It can be a small one, either candle or battery lit.

- Images and symbols from the "Freedom Quilts." (See the later chapter on The Quilt Codes of Freedom for more about these.)

- A toy gun. Some of us do include replicas or toy guns on her shrine. She carried a revolver for much of her conductor days, as well as brandished a musket during the Civil War. It's a tool that brought her safety and protection, and she was a warrior.

The Conjure Symbol for the Spirits of the Underground Railroad

The conjure symbol, or sigil for the spirits of the U.G.R.R., is based on the "Cairn and Cross," as the most common grave marker for freedom seekers. It is the seal that defines what much of the work with the spirits of the U.G.R.R. is about: supporting the work of giving peace to the literally thousands of souls who, like Harriet Tubman's Followers, have simply vanished as far as knowing who they are, what their stories entail, and where they have been laid to rest. As of the writing of this book it has been in use for seventeen years. At this point it has been used by countless practitioners in their own way to connect with, invoke, and commune with the U.G.R.R. spirits, whether Mama Moses and those we know like Frederick Douglass, John Brown, Sojourner Truth, Thomas Garrett, and John W. Jones or those we only learn about in working with the spirit realm.

- We see in the sigil a cairn and cross, which is the most basic and common style of grave marker that many freedom seekers, who either perished while struggling for freedom or even those that made it to Canada, were buried under. First a hill of rocks would be piled over the buried body. Then this would be adorned with a humble cross. Even those who made it to freedom could afford little more. Sadly, these grave markers are not built to withstand time. So even in plots we know house the bodies of the once enslaved—both the free or those who died trying—the cairns and crosses were easily damaged or desecrated, or succumbed to Father Time himself. This is why we resurrect and build them—on the land and in sigils.

- We see the cross itself: a Christian symbol containing religious mysteries as pertains to conjure. The cross connects above and below, Heaven and Hell, with our earth as the intermediary. The cross is a literal crossroads, tying our world to the world of spirit—whether it be up, down, right, left, or all around.

- We see the rocks piled in formation, an homage to the cannonball formation upon the Haitian flag, which reads "L'Union Fait La Force," Unity Makes Strength. The Haitian Revolution was inspiration to many of the enslaved in the Americas, as well as inspiring John Brown and his eventual insurrection.

- We see in the sigil the waning moon, in this case in its last quarter. This is the mysterious and potent part of the moon's phases associated with "the Crone" and her mysteries in witchcraft. Mama Moses is often depicted as a crone: an older "wise woman" possessing ancient magic and wisdom, honored as a sacred strength and power in witchcraft. Many photos were taken of her in her later years. Although I see her manifest, as do others, as a younger woman—fit and formidable at times as General Tubman—she is most assuredly well-represented in photos as the Crone in all her power. The last quarter of the moon is the time to wield what some refer to as "dark magic." The U.G.R.R. was a dark entity and illegal in its time. It was considered nefarious, thieving, and hostile to slavers and those who supported them. The tactics of survival and success for the U.G.R.R. indeed invoked death, whether for defense or retribution; blood was spilled and spilled often. The magic of the conjurers on the Railroad, as well as to this day, is still considered nefarious by some. The rootworkers of the U.G.R.R. enlisted spirits and threw tricks for dumbing and cursing masters, overseers, and bounty hunters alike. Charms and spells had to be used at times upon the freedom seekers' own people, those that were not to be trusted or sadly loyal to the master and willing to betray those about to steal away. Charms of invisibility and track hiding had to be utilized at all stages of a break for freedom. On a pragmatic level, the last quarter of the moon was the most beneficial time for freedom seekers and conductors alike to travel and work the tracks of the U.G.R.R. in the blessed darkness the phase offered.

- We see in the sigil the Big Dipper: the seven stars that make up the constellation Ursa Major, aka the Great Bear. In U.G.R.R. code this was referred to as the Drinking Gourd, the great clue and companion in the sky pointing the way to the North Star. A gourd had many meanings to the African and their eventual descendants in bondage, not only as a hollowed vessel to drink from, but as a place to carry herbs, roots, and medicine as a type of "charm" and form of carrier magic. Harriet Tubman was said to have a gourd upon her for "carrying the charm." In our tradition the Drinking Gourd is also called the "Cup of Conjure" encapsulating its many mysteries.

- We see in the sigil the North Star above the cross, the veritable symbol of the Underground Railroad. The North Star, Polaris, is unique in that it has a fixed position in the night sky and has been used for navigation around the world and through the ages. Frederick Douglass's newsletter which shed light upon the horrors of slavery, supported those who helped fight it, and shared news of all kinds for and about the abolitionist movement was called The North Star. The North Star was the guiding light for those that would steal away and make their break for freedom. It was housed within mysteries and coded spirituals as part of the Big Dipper constellation that was referred to as the Drinking Gourd and the Cup of Conjure. Thousands found their way via the North Star, praying to it, singing to it, and making it part of their conjurations to freedom. It is still sacred to those that revere the spirits of the U.G.R.R., a gate and doorway to the ancestors of this spirit world. It is a place that we look to at night when we conjure and call forth Mama Moses and her Followers, a celestial mirror where the elevated spirits of the U.G.R.R. manifest as well as rest in the heavens. When we look up to the North Star during our conjures, we too are blessed by its sacred light, inspiration, and guidance. In the sigil the North Star is the Hebrew Star of David, in homage to Harriet Tubman as the Moses of her people, as well as to the underrated contributions of the Jewish people in the Americas integral to the abolitionist movement.

- The symbol in the midsection of the cross is a combination of the "Square and Compasses" of Masonry and the "vevè," a sacred symbol with many mysteries used in predominantly Haitian vodou. The Square and Compasses represent the Prince Hall Masons, the Black Masonic Lodge that was founded by a free man of color named Prince Hall, along with fourteen other free men of color prior to the American War of Independence. They too were integral in the fight against slavery and formed part of the Underground Railroad before it even had a name. The Prince Hall Masons were founded upon the ideals of liberty, equality, and peace. The vodou vevè is for the Marassa: ancient and sacred spirits known as the Lwa who manifest as divine twins. There were indeed many who were enslaved in Louisiana, and in New Orleans in particular, that walked the freedom trails all the way to St. Catharines, Ontario. Their stories and names are preserved in academic slave narratives. Some of those very travelers who put down roots in St. Catharines were dedicated adherents to their vodou and drew upon their spirituality in many ways to serve themselves, as well as their fellow freedom seekers on their harrowing journeys that took at times upward of two years.

The Followers of Mama Moses bestowed and revealed the mysteries of this sigil to me, guiding my hands upon entering my home a mere block from the BME Church in St. Catharines, at the end of Tubman's track of the Underground Railroad.

Working with the Cairn and Cross

While it's perfectly fine to print out a copy of the conjure symbol and use it in any size desired, I recommend that before using it you at least draw it out a few times. This will help you navigate the sigil and begin to make an imprint in your mind of some of its mysteries that will remain hidden until they have been experienced. It is best to draw it out on paper first to get a feel for it and its paths.

There really is no set place in the sigil to begin from. Each time a different person creates it, it's a different personal journey and mystery. Over the years it has been digitally printed, painted, chalked onto floors and walls, embroidered, set down with cascarilla powder, drawn into dirt, and even laid out in cornmeal upon the earth. There is no harm or foul in using a ruler, compass, or any other tool you see fit to execute it as cleanly as you can. When you begin to draw one out to use in either a ritual or on your altar, make that a moment and magic in and of itself.

- Take the time to stop and center yourself.

- Contemplate what you are about to create.

- Light a candle to bring illumination to your work.

- Say aloud and from the heart that you are creating this Cairn and Cross sigil in honor of Mama Moses and the spirits of the Underground Railroad—to help them navigate to you and to show them that you are a friend.

- While drawing it out, let yourself get lost in the process as best you can.

- When it is done, stop again and ponder the process you just underwent.

It's always best to apply this procedure pretty much every time you create this symbol in whatever fashion you choose. Later in the book we will learn how to build an actual Cairn and Cross this sigil represents.

The Freedom Seeker

The "Freedom Seeker" was the first runner on the trails of freedom; a scout, guide, messenger, and playful trickster. He was also a conjurer. As the first of his people to navigate the trails of the U.G.R.R., he was charged with keeping the magic of Africa contained in his satchel. His stick is a sacred African branch. He created the U.G.R.R. in the minds of his people, inspired it, showed it was possible. It was he that revealed the paths, the stars, the Cup of Conjure sitting high in the sky. It was he that planted those mysteries that took root, for he was the first American rootworker, the first American conjurer. Some of the Gullah people started a game with him—carried on to this day. When he is glimpsed in the night, they say aloud, "Seen!" His name is a mystery, a trick, the first code to exist: Ras—Run Away Slave.

At just about every U.G.R.R. historic site, church, cemetery, and trail you will find an image of the Freedom Seeker—whether in silhouette, painted, or on signage. He is the head of an entire freedom seeker court of spirits known as the Followers. He was a spirit running the trails since its beginning, elevated and invoked since those early days, and on many an occasion he helped guide Mama Moses and her train. He is one of the strongest and kindest spirits that is hidden in plain sight, a most tangible spirit that is enabled and empowered every time his image is created or placed in prominence across the North American continent—from churches to museums, roads to homes, books to statues. Even for those that have no idea who he truly is and would never condone the image or mark of a spirit, that is the trick he plays. I am not the only witchdoctor to be scorned and scolded for sorcery by a preacher, while Ras laughingly adorns the very house of prayer behind the blowhards.

Some say he is the image of High John the Conqueror, and well, sometimes he is. He plays tricks on many. But for those of us who work among and for the spirits of the U.G.R.R., he is our friend, our guide, and our messenger.

Ras the Freedom Seeker will accept any and all offerings placed among any and all spirits of the U.G.R.R. He will be your guide and your friend for as long as you revere and honor the spirits of the U.G.R.R., for he runs still to this day, looking for those lost and left behind. His spirit travels from image to image, altar to shrine no matter where they are placed; they are his doorways and mark his trails. From churches to voodoo temples, homes to graveyards, wherever his image is placed in any fashion he will have entrance. If you ask him to curse, he will laugh at you, and you will find yourself crossed in ways that no amount of cleansing baths will fix—you will simply be fixed. Adorn your shrine with his image, give him a door to your home, and light a candle for him. He will only bring good magic, news, laughter, and blessings for honoring the spirit world he birthed and protects.

His name is Ras and he will also answer to "Freedom Seeker," but I recommend that you do not call him "runaway slave" or refer to him or any of the U.G.R.R. spirits as "slave." You will notice that throughout this book I only use the term "slave" for descriptive purposes within a certain context. The Africans were not slaves: they were prisoners, and not very agreeable ones who fought continually against their bondage. It goes without saying that referring to any of these spirits as a slave or slaves is an insult and degrades their beautiful souls, power, and legacy.

Prayer for the Freedom Seeker

Your interactions with Ras will change and become more personal the more you work with and recognize him. Guided by your own intuition and time spent with him and his fellow spirits, you will feel the tangible nature of his presence change over time as well as after creating an altar or shrine to Mama Moses and the Followers and exploring the other mysteries within these pages. If you create a space for him or place his image in a doorway in any manner, the prayer and words of invocation are the same.

Freedom Seeker, Ras, I call to you, I offer my shrine and home for you.

I give you another doorway, open another road for you to travel.

Ras, I am a friend (if you are African American, you can say you are kin and blood), guard my home and guide my work as I honor you and your legacy, revering Mama Moses and the Followers.

My home and work will always be to illuminate and sustain you and the spirits of the U.G.R.R., and this space is always for you to visit.

I bid you love and Godspeed!

Look for Ras among your conjurations and invocations, and when you build the Cairn and Cross. When you glimpse him out of the side of your eye, play the game he enjoys and say aloud, "Seen!"

Offerings for Mama Moses

When you want to make a serious connection, then sustaining offerings will take the connection to the next tangible level. Fresh foods and liquids she was fond of have an energy that can give Mama Moses strength. The energy of food as well as the aromas that permeate the air in both the human and spirit world are an attractive and tantalizing offering that can empower a spirit on another level. A food offering demonstrates to the spirit world that you have taken the time and sacrifice to honor them with foods that they enjoyed while they walked with the living. It also keeps them present longer as you honor or petition them with your needs. Making a sustaining offering is also a good practice after receiving or recognizing blessings from the spirits. If you have asked Mama Moses and her Followers for spiritual help, and it indeed appears, then a thank-you meal/offering shows gratitude for the blessing bestowed.

Some food offerings will last longer than others. Fruit and vegetables in particular can last on an altar or shrine for weeks, actually, but it is best to clear away cooked food within a day and especially once it is no longer fresh. When a food offering has become hard or stale, or is about to become rotten, remove it from the shrine—preferably before any of those things take place. I personally like to leave such offerings outside in nature once I remove them from the altar as opposed to placing them in the trash.

Particular sustainable offers for Mama Moses include the following:

- Corn bread, or hoe cake as Mama Moses referred to it in life. Mama Moses was known to be a connoisseur and critic of corn breads brought to her as gifts. It was one of her favorite foods.

- Tea with butter. This was a favorite of Mama Moses to drink and enjoy.

- Coffee. Hot black coffee was a delicacy of sorts for Mama Moses; it brought comfort and represented rest and safety. It was a drink that meant communion among colleagues and conversation.

- Bread and small cakes.

- Yams/sweet potatoes.

- Pawpaws, if you can find them. This fruit is not readily available in stores, but these trees in the apple family grow in the eastern United States and southeastern Canada in temperate climates. This unique and indigenous North American fruit tree was once commonly found along waterways, rivers, and lands surrounding swamps. In the late summer and early autumn when pawpaw fruit is ripe, it was not only life-saving and valuable sustenance for the traveler, but a delicious delicacy. It is celebrated to this day and known by the folk names "Quakers delight" and "hillbilly mango."

- Soft fruits such as oranges, grapes, bananas, and papayas

- Any warm food. Soups or stews of soft texture when cooked may be presented to her on special occasions, as well as soft fruits, which will bring favor and pleasure.

- Flowers of any kind in water for their life force, beauty, and sentiment.

- Alcohol is not recommended as an offering to Mama Moses. She was not fond of alcohol nor its effects on folks, although she was reportedly not harsh on her colleagues and friends who did enjoy it. It just wasn't one of her things. It's actually a common misconception that alcohol is a staple offering for *all* spirits associated with voodoo and conjure. It does indeed please many, but not Mama Moses specifically, nor would it please any spirit that had no love for it when living. However, when her spirit arrives, she does not always come alone, so it's okay to have small bottles of liquor or alcohol for her extended spiritual court, just not to present directly to her.

The Conjures of Mama Moses

Once you have cleansed, assembled, and arranged your space to honor Mama Moses, it's time to consecrate and dedicate it to her and her Followers.

Consecrating the Altar

- Take some time to breathe, center your mind, and concentrate on the work about to begin. Envision Mama Moses; contemplate her unique spirit and your space that is about to be dedicated to her.

- Light a taper candle and hold it in front of you for a few minutes, letting yourself be illuminated, as you are about to approach and consecrate your space.

- Light the jar candle with your taper, and extinguish the taper and place the jar candle on the altar or shrine. Or you can keep your taper lit and place it in a holder. As you do so, recite out loud,

    I light this candle to praise Harriet "Mama Moses""Tubman,
    to illuminate the way for Mama Moses and her Followers,
    a guiding light from the living to the dead.

- Hold up the glass of water, moving it to make a cross in front of you. Then pass it through the cross you made just before you set it down, reciting,

    I offer the water of life to Mama Moses and her Followers,
    a gift from the living to the dead.

- Hold up some fruit, moving it to make a cross in front of you. Pass it though the cross you made just before you set it down and recite,

    I offer this food to you, Mama Moses, may it strengthen and please you and
    your Followers. Praise be Mama Moses.

- Go on to recite,

I consecrate this space to the pure and holy spirit of Harriet "Mama Moses"
Tubman, I dedicate this place to Mama Moses and her Followers.
This is a place for love, reverence, and the memory of those good souls that
were supporters, conductors, and travelers of the Underground Railroad.
May this place always be one of love, blessings, and honor for Mama Moses
and all that she stood for. Praise be Mama Moses.

- Knock or gently stomp three times slowly on any surrounding or
  facing surface, and call forth:

General Tubman, General Tubman, General Tubman.

Mama Moses, to your glory and strength I have dedicated this space.

Nana Tubman, bless this place with your power and compassion.

This guiding flame is for you and your Followers.

This water is for you and your Followers.

This food is for you and your Followers.

Mama Moses, this place is a safe house and sacred space for you
and your Followers.

May your spirit always be welcome here while you travel
to those that call to you.

May my work with you expand and strengthen your powerful spirit.

Mama Moses, I ask that as long as your sacred beacon, the North
Star, shines from above, I will be blessed by your gifts
as I nurture and honor your holy spirit.

Praise be to you, Mama Moses.

- Next read from the Book of Exodus to please Mama Moses:

And Moses said unto God, Who am I, that I should go unto Pharaoh, and that I should bring forth the children of Israel out of Egypt? And he said, Certainly I will be with thee; and this shall be a token unto thee, that I have sent thee: When thou hast brought forth the people out of Egypt, ye shall serve God upon this mountain.

- Recite, or sing if you are familiar with the tune, the spiritual "Go Down Moses":

When Israel was in Egypt's land, / Let my people go,

Oppress'd so hard they could not stand, / Let my People go.

Go down, Moses, / Way down in Egypt's land,

Tell old Pharaoh, / Let my people go.

Oh let us on to Canaan go, let my people go,

What a beautiful morning that will be, let my people go,

When time breaks up in eternity, let my people go

Go down, Moses, / Way down in Egypt's land,

Tell old Pharaoh, / Let my people go.

- Finish off by saying, "Mama Moses, may this space dedicated to you bring your spirit joy and show my dedication to your legacy. In love I bid you praise and Godspeed."

- Let the candle burn for a while and meditate on what you have worked. Gaze into her picture, gaze into the flame, and listen and let what you have just conjured, wielded, and manifested fill your soul. Recognize and remember the feeling it brought to call to her, recite for her, and consecrate an altar for Mama Moses. This is a good beginning to forging your connection and sanctifying your workspace.

The crossing motion with food and drink offerings is to make a door to spirit, and then you pass these items through the door as a gift for the spirits. While any motion in the air that resonates with you including a pentagram could be used in theory, the traditional motion is to make the cross. When we bid Mama Moses Godspeed, we do so in homage to the blessing said among the many friends, supporters, and travelers of the U.G.R.R.

STANDARD PRAYER AND PETITION TO MAMA MOSES

This prayer is one that has been in use for many years. You will find it on prayer cards and shared among those who work with the spirits of the U.G.R.R. It can be utilized anywhere at any time within any of her conjurations.

General Tubman, General Tubman, General Tubman!

Mama Moses, who led so many to freedom,

I ask for your blessings and powers to unshackle me from that which binds me. Free me of those obstacles that hinder my growth.

Bless me, Mama Moses, as I gaze upon the North Star, your celestial gate and shining mystery, always present in the night sky.

May my roads always lead to freedom and may I never be crossed.

Lend me your powers of healing and perseverance, cunning and conjure.

May peace always be upon you and your followers, may my prayers be heard, praise be Mama Moses and Godspeed!

You can place items upon the altar space you created for Mama Moses to ask for a blessing upon them and then carry them on your person for a host of blessings and connection. The following ritual is to empower a High John the Conqueror root for protection.

- Place a piece of High John the Conqueror root on your altar to Mama Moses.

- Leave it there for a day or so to absorb the energy of your shrine.

- When you are ready or it is needed, light up the altar by candle flame and consecrate the root.

- Knock three times and call forth to Mama Moses:

    General Tubman, General Tubman, General Tubman,

    I ask for you to envelop me in your protection in this time of need.

    Mama Moses, I ask that but a ray of your holy light stays with me and protects my body and spirit.

    Empower High John the Conqueror to aid and carry your blessings upon me.

- Now speak of the issue you need protection from.

- Pick up the piece of High John root, clutch it in your hands, and place it to your heart while you recite:

Mama Moses, be ever present in my time of need. Let High John carry your light. Praise be to you, Mama Moses, and Godspeed.

- Breathe onto the High John root, tap it three times, and say:

    Awaken and remember your power.

- Clutching the root, recite:

High John the Conqueror, powerful spirit of protection, prince of conjure,
empower your sacred root and let it hold the holy light of Mama Moses.

Have a little bottle of whiskey at hand. It can be as small as the airplane-size bottles; a tiny bit will do. Incidentally, whiskey is the most traditional libation and offering made to spirits and roots by hoodoo and conjure workers of North America, at least until a certain era. With many ATRs and their practices proliferating in recent decades as well as being misappropriated, certain nuances have been lost over time for certain conjure formulas, and rum, which was the Caribbean tradition's libation of choice, has overshadowed whiskey. When it comes to High John root, the legacy offering is whiskey.

- Take a small sip of the whiskey and then spray it onto the root from your mouth. This is the traditional way to feed the root as you share your essence with it. However, if this is not possible for you, you can drip some onto the root instead. We will go into this more in the chapter for High John the Conqueror.

- Let the root dry as you continue to clutch it and say again, now to High John, what it is you need protection from.

- Place the root in your pocket and carry it on you for as long as the protection is needed. (For this basic work it is not necessary to wrap the root in material, but there will be more on this later.)

This can be done for many forms of protection, whether in your home, at work, or for your general environment and people you are not comfortable with as well as for safeguarding your surroundings psychically. Just be specific when describing the situation you need protection from in your petition. This can of course be repeated as often as needed. (For more on High John and working with his spirit, see the chapter on High John the Conqueror, the Prince of Conjure.)

Nameless Followers, St. Catharines, circa 1850s, Rick Bell Family Fonds

Adding in Those Who Travel with Mama Moses: The Followers

You'll notice that we've mentioned "Followers" a few times and called upon them in the consecration of the altar for Mama Moses. The Followers are the spiritual court of Mama Moses. These spirits for the most part have no names but surround her as helpers and protectors. They are also called the "Freedom Seekers," but these are distinct from Ras, the Freedom Seeker we heard about in the last chapter. They are the spirits of those that ran ahead as scouts in her days as a conductor. They are the ones that would help her with reading and correspondence, for Harriet Tubman never learned to read or write and had trusted confidants for such things. They are the ones that were so grateful for her helping them gain their freedom and live a life they otherwise would not have been able to have, they vowed to serve her in this life and the next. Many are healers, warriors, diviners, preachers, and rootworkers, or else they are the random spirits that fought for their freedom, made the trek, but sadly perished along the way, now aligned with those in the afterlife that have chosen to serve from the U.G.R.R. spirit world.

We honor and work with these spirits at length. Although we do not know their names, trust that there are no malignant or harmful spirits of any kind in close proximity to Mama Moses. Her holy spirit travels and manifests with only those blessed by their god who labored toward equality and justice, and although they were subjected to the horrors of slavery, she indeed had friends that were of many colors and religions while they walked the tracks of freedom.

Her Followers in many cases arrive at shrines, rituals, and workings ahead of Mama Moses to ascertain the surroundings and assess the ones calling to her. They ensure that her spirit will only answer to calls for blessings and reverence but never curses. Her Followers often include a runner or scout, faith healers, bodyguards, diviners, rootworkers, and at times a preacher. When it is said that Mama Moses does not always come alone, these are the spirits I refer to.

The Followers bear resemblance to other families or "nations" of spirits found in some of the African traditional religions. There are similarities between her Followers and La Madama of Santeria and Espiritismo. La Madama encompasses women who, when living, were enslaved or were descendants of slaves in Cuba and Puerto Rico. They were practitioners of Santeria or Espiritismo when alive and also healers and diviners. They are most often portrayed with the image of a house servant from the 1800s: wearing aprons and gingham skirts with their hair wrapped in cloth. There are many different types of La Madama spirits enlisted for many reasons by those within that tradition.

Another family of spirits that bear resemblance to the Followers is the Preto Velho ("old black man") and Preta Velha ("old black woman") of Afro-Brazilian Umbanda. They too are spirits that were once enslaved and for their part died so. Because of their life in enslavement, they are considered by Umbanda adherents as the ones with the most compassion and understanding when it comes to pain and suffering. They are beloved spirits, and many of them, when alive, were Yoruba priests, healers, and diviners. They are portrayed and manifest in plain white garments, straw hats, and head wraps.

The Followers in some instances also bear a resemblance to the nation of spirits in Haitian vodou known as the Guédé (pronounced gede). The Guédé are "Lwa," spirits of the dead who travel and manifest, broken up into their own various branches and courts. The Guédé are often portrayed as skeletal beings with many different personalities and attributes, wearing top hats and other colorful modes of dress based on the nation they belong to. They are for the most part celebratory, if not a little raucous, but they do have their complexities. The Guédé are beloved and honored spirits.

So as we can see, the Followers of Mama Moses resemble other spirit families that shared similar lives. Whereas these others are from the Caribbean, South America, and their cultural legacies, the Followers are North America's spirits of warriors, rootworkers, healers, and diviners, and this is profound. When it comes to statuary and effigies for altars, since La Madama and Preto Velho statues are easily found in botanicas across North America, we can use them to decorate our U.G.R.R. shrines as symbols for the Followers as they are similar in their dress, attire, and look to many of the Freedom Seeker spirits of the Underground Railroad.

The Followers are the ones who will accept alcohol as offerings. Shrines built for Mama Moses often hold bottles of liquor at the ends of the altar or on the floor/ground beside or in front of it. They will also partake in any offerings left for Mama Moses and her "Followers." Also, if you feel the call to elaborate on offerings to include these spirits, they will gladly accept hard candy, corn, and apples—foods that otherwise would have been uncommon for Mama Moses to enjoy or eat. So when her altar is created, it's always good to think of her Followers and honor them with their own tools if space permits. Such tools are as follows:

- A machete, buck knife, or blade of any sort

- A pipe and tobacco

- Roots, oils, or herbs associated with healing, conjure, and rootwork, such as High John and Dixie John root, devil's shoestring, hyssop oil

- African or Caribbean statues, carvings, or masks

- A walking cane or wooden staff

- A broom, to honor those many that "jumped the broom" in the symbolic and spiritual wedding that was the way for many of the enslaved. It is also a tool for magic, placed above doorways and used to banish bad juju.

- Dice, dominoes, or playing cards. Many of these spirits enjoyed playing with these in life, and they still bring enjoyment in spirit.

- Cowrie shells, small animal bones (chicken bones will more than suffice), or small animal skulls. These were used for divination and to enhance animal spirit magic that many performed.

- Flowers in a water-filled glass or vase

- An image of the Freedom Seeker

- Images or re-creations of the Freedom Quilt symbols

- A gun. Others and myself again include a replica or toy rifle for the Followers, as that was what some of them carried for hunting and protection.

- Straw hats or felt bowlers. These are enjoyed as accoutrements in spirit as they were in life.

- Replica or decorative human skulls and various sized coffins. All of my shrines or altars built for Mama Moses and her Followers include these. While that may seem a bit macabre for some, they are fitting after all for the sacred dead.

Once you have worked with this spirit world a bit, you will be able to differentiate between the presence of Mama Moses and that of her Followers. You will be able to feel them arrive shortly before her and leave shortly after, and you will be able to tell the difference in time, as you get more comfortable. The reason or purpose you have called to Mama Moses will often determine who accompanies her, and you will be able to identify and recognize which of her Followers is responding. There will come a time when you may work solely with them, and that's when you will also really be able to start to see them as individuals. When that happens, the relationship can become very close.

These spirits are the ones that first presented themselves to me when I began my work with the U.G.R.R. spirit world and were integral in guiding me to Mama Moses and bringing her to myself and many others. They are beneficial, beautiful, and powerful spirits. Let's get to know some of their manifestations and explore deeper workings with Mama Moses and her Followers.

Connecting to the Diviners

Both Mama Moses and some of those spirits in her court are diviners. If you are not set in your ways already with guides for divination and want to expand or explore the blessings the Followers can share or you are just beginning to hone your divining skills, then I would encourage you to petition the spirits for extra potency toward your craft.

This can be done by placing your divination tools upon the altar or shrine to Mama Moses and her Followers, whether these are tarot cards, runes, bones, or shells. Let them rest there for a day or so. As well, place a separate jar candle with them that will later be utilized in your divination, so it can charge and absorb energy from the shrine.

- Light up the altar to Mama Moses and her Followers

- Call forth to the spirits, knocking three times:

*General Tubman, Mama Moses, and those in your court
that are the diviners,*

I ask for your blessings and magic of seership.

Empower, manifest, and bless my tools.

Help guide, guard, and protect as I divine and conjure.

Be ever present as I gaze into the mysteries.

Help me see what must be seen, to help those who need to know.

- Sprinkle a few drops of water on your tools from the glass on the shrine, anointing them with the blessed water of life.

- Take the candle for future divination and say: "Mama Moses and your Diviners, may this candle be your guiding light; may it illuminate and enhance my work. To Mama Moses and the Diviners, I bid you love and Godspeed."

- Each time you use your tools, light the divination candle no matter where you are, and ask for the Diviners to manifest and aid in your work.

This is a very effective way to get to know and build a relationship with the diviners in Mama Moses's court. You will soon come to know and recognize one in particular that has chosen to work with you, and this can present itself in numerous ways. You may feel this spirit's presence, and this is not something to be feared. You may even catch glimpses of them through your peripheral vision or hear their words spoken; one of the benefits of this spirit world is that an overwhelming number of them spoke the English language to some degree when living, albeit not quite the way we use it today. You may notice their presence by aroma, catching the scent of certain fragrances not based in your location. You may also recognize the way their chosen candle burns or feel that divination is coming in unregular clarity. Finally, you may see, hear, and be visited by them in your dreams or meditations—something that you will have to verify as it comes as all part of a unique process common in the occult.

Build that relationship as best you can by expressing your gratitude for their aid and manifestation, thanking them after every reading, feeding them as often as you can, and being sure there is water or liquor at the table just for them when you call and divine. You may eventually come to dedicate a particular statue or effigy in your shrine for the Diviners or place a new one there just for this purpose. This will be one you can take with you and place with your divination candle, water, and any other libation wherever and whenever you divine. This will become a beneficial, personal, and powerful connection to a spirit within the court of Mama Moses that will continue to grow with time. It is quite possible that one of the Diviners appears to be the spirit of a person of European descent or white; we will explore that later in the chapter on the court of spirits called the Spiritualists.

Mama Moses and the Healers

In the court that surrounds Mama Moses, there are also unique spirits that were faith healers during their time on earth: those who would call down the Holy Spirit, laying of hands upon the body, and invoke divine intervention through chant and prayer on behalf of the sick and maligned. They were for the most part women, Evangelicals and Baptists, and travelers of the U.G.R.R. Many Baptists traveled the U.G.R.R. from numerous locations in the southern United States and arrived in St. Catharines. Their numbers were significant enough that they built the historic Zion Baptist Church, just a few hundred feet from the BME Church that was the house of prayer for Harriet Tubman. Faith healers were ever present in the Zion Baptist congregation up until recent times. Mama Moses too was known to use a form of "laying hands" in some of her healings, both when she was a conductor and later a nurse tending to fevers during the Civil War. Whether she was calling heaven down in conjure or through the power of the Holy Spirit no one knows, but this skill was part of her legacy as a mystic with the "charm."

You might call upon the Healers for several reasons: for healing of physical, emotional, or spiritual needs. When petitioning the Healers, it is best to make an offering of food and fresh water. These will strengthen and sustain them for the work. For healings, some fresh fruit of at least a couple of varieties is best, as well as flowers of any kind for helping with the work by adding in their life force.

- Place an extra glass of water on the shrine for yourself.

- Light up the altar for Mama Moses: cleanse the space and light her candle.

- For the Healers, it is good to light at least three or more candles for the extra "heat"—both as a beacon and for the power the flames can produce.

- Present your offerings to the shrine in the manner described previously, making the cross motion before placement.

- Light a white taper candle, and hold it in front of you with one hand with a Bible in the other. Stay like this for a few moments. You are approaching and calling to sacred spirits of faith healers, so let yourself be illuminated in the glow.

- Call forth to Mama Moses and her Followers:

  Mama Moses, Mama Moses, Mama Moses!

  General Tubman, I call to you and your healers.

  Nana Tubman, I call to you and your faith healers.

- Recite or sing:

  Come Down, O Love Divine,

  Seek thou this soul of mine,

  Healers visit it with thine own
  love glowing.

  O Comforters, draw near,

  Within my heart appear,
  and kindle it, with thy holy flame,

  Heal me Healers, in Glory's name.

- Optionally now recite the Lord's Prayer.

- At this point place the taper candle in a holder, and arrange yourself in a comfortable position—whether sitting down or, if possible, lying down—being ever aware of your connection to the altar.

- Once you are comfortable, place the Bible on your body, if possible somewhere connected to your affliction, and close your eyes and call to them again:

  Mama Moses, I ask for you and your Healers to lay your hands upon me.
  Help heal me of that which ails me.

- Say this over again in your mind a couple of times with your eyes closed, yet still connected to the shrine.

- Envision Mama Moses and her Healers gathered about you, laying their hands upon the part of you that requires their touch.

- Envision your entire being awash in their holy light, glowing in sacred illumination.

- Focus on the part of your body or spirit needing the healing touch.

- Let Mama Moses and her Healers fill your mind, body, and soul with their sacred light, placing their holy hands upon you.

- Let this process continue for as long as possible. Try to enter a meditative state or even sleep. Let yourself rest in the embrace of Mama Moses and her Followers as they lay hands upon you.

- When you feel the connection has passed and that the work is over or you awaken from your semi- or unconscious state, open your eyes but stay still and silent while your awareness returns to ordinary reality.

- When you are ready, approach the altar and thank the spirits, still holding the Bible:

Mama Moses, Healers of spirit,

I thank you for your holy touch.

Blessings of love to you Mama Moses!

I offer gratitude to Mama Moses and her Followers.

Godspeed!

- Finish off by drinking the water you placed upon the altar for yourself. Put the Bible back on the altar.

You can add to this rite in ways you may feel empower it even more. This can be done by lighting several candles if the space permits and laying them out around you or where you may be laying down. As with most of the conjures for the spirits of the U.G.R.R., your intuition will undoubtedly come into play and inspire you to contribute that which may enhance your work with the spirits.

Working with a Bible

It's a good practice to cleanse whatever Bible you choose to use for your shrine and for the healings—making it a personal tool for you and your work with the spirits. Cleansing your Bible is similar to cleansing your altar space, just slightly different semantics. You can cleanse your Bible by immersing it in any incense smoke, holding it so that you can open the various pages and let them be purified with smoke. You can also anoint it with Florida Water or Hoyt's Cologne, even sprinkling tiny amounts throughout the pages. This can also be done with an oil for purposes of cleansing, even if it has been commercially purchased. While cleansing your Bible and making it yours, don't underestimate your own power and magic to banish, if you will, some of the older residue that was someone else's as you personalize it. Know that many older ones easily found already possess a unique residue of "mana" or supernatural power through prayer, and your cleansing will not remove this unless you will it.

Once cleansed, you can anoint it—a baptismal, if you will, to now claim it as a magical tool. This can be done using any oil for blessing purposes, like hyssop or sage (as well as the Jerusalem oil we'll cover shortly). Rub some on the front and back cover, making any symbol you feel inclined to and saying: "I seal my work and anoint thee mine." This should suffice in finishing up your work.

If you are not fond of the Bible, consider the work with the spirits as a time for you explore it as a crossover tool for magic. Until I began my work with the U.G.R.R. spirits, I was a person who would never have considered using a Bible for any reason and actually tried to rationalize not doing so, resisting it at every turn. But I am beyond grateful that I was able to learn to work with one on my own terms for the purposes at hand. It was a unique blessing in and of itself from the compassionate spirits.

Petitioning the Healers

Petitioning the Healers to aid another person, be it a friend or family, is done in a similar manner.

Approach the altar in the same way as before, preferably with the same offerings you would use for your own healing. It's pretty much a given that you should have permission from the recipient that it's okay to send the Healers to their side. Only if they happen to be too sick to be conscious will it be more than acceptable to send the Healers if you feel it is a necessity or could add to the healing they need, but never send them to a person who is sad, emotional, or hurt unless you have permission to do so. The Healers themselves will not be pleased, nor Mama Moses, to work for a person that does not want their help. You can either do this work for the agreeable recipient at your own inclination or availability, or at a preplanned time when your recipient can also relax and participate to a degree from distance—whatever seems to be best will be good.

Light the taper candle, hold the Bible, and call them forth. Once you have petitioned them, place the Bible back on the altar, only now if possible with a photo of your recipient or their name written out on paper within the pages. For some, choosing certain sections of the Bible to place the photo can also be effective. For example, for a physical ailment you could place the recipient's name or photo at Jeremiah 30:17: "'But I will restore you to health and heal your wounds,' declares the Lord." If the problem is emotional or spiritual in nature, you could choose John 14:27: "Peace I leave with you; my peace I give you. I do not give to you what the world gives. Do not let your hearts be troubled and do not be afraid."

- For the duration of the work, hold on to the taper with both hands, with that being your focus.

- Ask Mama Moses and the Healers to travel to your desired recipient in need, and tell them the name of the person seeking the healing and what ails them.

- Once you feel the connection to the Healers, close your eyes and focus your thoughts on the recipient, envisioning Mama Moses and her Healers surrounding your loved one as they lay hands upon them and illuminate them with sacred light. You are the conduit between your recipient and the Healers; let the candle you hold be that connection.

- Keep strong the vision of your recipient as the Healers heal, for as long as you can.

- When you feel the work has been completed, open your eyes and thank the spirits as before. Place the taper candle still lit upon the altar and let it burn for a while longer as you ponder your working and return to ordinary reality.

Bear in mind these healing rituals can be done for circumstances relating to emotional and spiritual needs as well as a physical ailment. Use your discretion, and know that there is no reason not to ask for healing for such types of distress. If you feel help is necessary and are compelled to call to them, make the offerings, petition the Healers, and thank them for their holy light.

The Machete

One tool synonymous with not only many uprisings but also the U.G.R.R. is the machete. The machete is a farm and work tool, the most basic instrument for cutting away debris, but it has also served other purposes: as a sacrificial blade on livestock and more definitively as a weapon. As a weapon the machete is the equalizer of the poor, the indentured, and the enslaved. When I facilitate ceremonies, at a certain point I hold up the machete and remind us all that somewhere on this planet, this year and every year, a tyrant or despot, whether regional or national, who possesses modern weaponry and the soldiers to use them, will be toppled by the will of a group of people armed with simple farm tools, featuring the machete.

Many of the slave uprisings in the Americas—some known to history and others not so much—were ones where the main weapon was the pragmatic and always available machete. For the enslaved in North America, this was in fact one of the only weapons available for protection. For those that fled for freedom, guns were a rarity. The machete is small and effective, and served not only as protection against wild animals and slavers but also as a tool of necessity for some of the harsh conditions a freedom seeker would have had to endure and travel through. The machete was the all-serving all-purpose tool. The machete can be our sacred tool used for a few purposes and is a recommended one in working among the spirits of the U.G.R.R.

Most magical, spiritual, and ceremonial traditions utilize a blade or blades for everything from casting to protection to ritualistic symbolism. Swords, knives, daggers, and ceremonial blades are commonplace in most traditions that I assume many who read this book are familiar with to some degree. Wicca and British Traditional Witchcraft have probably brought the sacred blade to the forefront more than most. Circles cast in witchcraft utilize a double-edged sword to surround the sacred area with protection. There is also the athame, a sacred double-edged blade used at the altar to either cast or for the blessing of the chalice and the blade. Upon many a witch's altar will be the boleen, the sharpened knife for food offerings or to cut various things, depending on the ritual at hand. All these blades are consecrated in their own way for their own separate purpose. In working with the spirits of the U.G.R.R., the machete is all these things in one: it is our sacred blade for protection and summoning, honoring and surrounding ourselves among the spirits housed in this book.

I suggest and highly recommend that you procure a machete to enhance and honor the work shared in these pages. They are fortunately available in many big-box stores in the camping or hunting section and are so reasonably priced it's actually hard to believe at times. As one who travels North America to present rituals and workshops, most of them U.G.R.R. conjure-related, I cannot always have a machete in tow, and so I have found procuring one in most cities is quite easy and quite cheap. If you want to find a high-quality and decorative machete, do so, by all means, but truly for our purposes a very reasonably priced one is more than good enough. It is making it your sacred tool that counts, and before we use our machete, we will go over my recommendations for consecrating, feeding, and honoring your blade. To myself and colleagues who use a machete in the way we do for this particular spirit work, the machete takes on its own presence and becomes an extension of your magic.

The formula and instructions for blessing, feeding, and utilizing the machete as a tool for working with the spirits of the U.G.R.R. do not violate any system or secret. What I share here is what I have been taught, given permission to share, or created for the purposes of getting to know a sacred blade, its use in magic, and how to enhance one's work with the spirits.

Feeding the Machete

Spraying your machete with liquor is a potent way to share your essence with it. At the very least it forges a strong connection between the machete and your spirit.

Liquor is recommended to feed steel tools and has a way of charging metal, feeding it as it becomes a living extension of your magic. For this work rum is best, but any alcohol will do. As well, any liquid will suffice if you are not able to consume alcohol. Water has its own life, as we know. The rustier the machete becomes, the more mana and magic it contains. It reveals its work; it reveals that the machete is absorbing the offerings. This is why a cheaper one is better to have, because they can rust quite quickly. The machete should not be babied. Use it as often as possible, whether in magical works and conjures or in any circumstance outdoors. The more it's used, the more powerful a tool it becomes. This is a pragmatic multipurpose tool, as they were for those that we honor in these works.

- Hold the machete up and out away from your face, take a swig of rum, and spray it from your mouth onto the blade, feeding both sides of the blade. This is good to do before any magical working or spiritual use, as well as anytime you feel compelled to give your machete a drink. You cannot feed your machete too often. If you cannot consume alcohol but can have it in your presence, pouring it onto the blade will also suffice.

Empowering the Machete in Outdoor Work

Place the machete into the ground, point stuck into the earth so that it is standing up.

- Take a small taper candle of any color, and melt the bottom and drip it onto the handle so that you can place the candle on top.

- While the machete is piercing the earth, the candle upon the handle signifies that the machete is "working" for you, that it is protecting you. It illuminates your blade in the light and blessings of the spirits as it draws up the powers of the earth. It's good at any outdoor working to have the machete illuminated and anchored in the ground.

Consecration of the Machete by the Earth and Moon

Certain traditions will undoubtedly recognize elements of this working. It is one I try to do as well as share and teach as often as possible when it comes to ceremonial and magical blades, and there is no reason why we cannot incorporate this into a way of consecrating the machete.

Pick a moon cycle that fits into your schedule, as well as the possible plans this might take to achieve. This may be a rite that is not possible for months on end, and that is okay; some things are worth waiting for and working toward. This may be something you can do at your own place of dwelling and backyard, some land/backyard that a friend or family has access to and agrees for you to use, or a plot of wild land you are familiar with and feel secure your machete won't be found and dug up by a random person. If none of these are available to you, let me share what I know several have done in the same circumstance. If you cannot bury the blade into the very earth itself, bring some earth to you. If you are living in a large city and land is scarce, colleagues I know have done this in their kitchen windowsills, apartment balconies, front or back porches, etc.—anywhere really that can handle a decent-size bucket, box, or container large enough for you to fill with some earth that you have hopefully been able to gather from anywhere ranging from a park to community garden or even from the side of the road or in a culvert. You will need to fill a bag of earth from one of those types of locations, bring it to your home, and place it in your container, saving room for your machete one placed inside. I'm going to gather you get the point from here, and just know that many have had to improvise for this and similar rites.

- Pick the full moon that is best for you to work with.

- Have a piece of cloth, material, or towel that will be able to wrap around your machete and cover it up.

- Take a small handheld or larger garden shovel, depending on terrain, plant it into the earth with love in your heart for the very earth itself, and dig a hole at least eight inches deep and wide enough for your machete when ready.

- Hold your machete toward the full moon. Aiming into the very middle of the moon, draw that moon energy into the machete, and say aloud that you wish for the moon's powers to be encapsulated into your blade. Really focus and draw the moon's light and power into your blade.

- Feed your machete with rum, allowing for the blade to glisten in the moon's light.

- Wrap the machete in the material, place it into the predug hole, and cover the hole and the machete with earth.

- Leave your machete buried for one whole moon cycle. While it is buried beneath the earth, it will gather magnetic nourishment, ancestral blessings from our past relations and ancestors laying beneath the very ground, and be charged by the earth, which can only make any ceremonial and ritual tool that much more potent. This is a blessing to bestow on a tool that will come to serve us in many works as well. Now the machete will become an extension of your own spirit and conjure work, and it will take on its own protective and obstacle-clearing presence. To bury the machete is indeed a ritual burial as found in most cultures of the world, at least where tribal magic and practices are concerned. It's a blessing for your tool to provide it with a ritual moon cycle burial, and the benefits will reveal themselves in no time upon completion. Potentially during that moon cycle you may want to probe your thoughts or listen to ones arriving, and consider giving your machete a "name" to personalize it even more.

- Next full moon, dig up and retrieve your machete.

- Unfurl the machete from the material, and feed it with rum.

- Hold it up to the full moon, again aiming into the very center of the moon and again drawing the moon's energy into it.

- Talk to your machete and welcome it back above the earth as it is charged and blessed by the moon. If a name has been chosen, this would be the time to announce that for your earth-charged blade.

- Pour an offering into the hole and recover it. Thank and honor the earth and ground about you. This can be any libation you feel is appropriate.

Your machete is now charged by the earth for an entire moon cycle—full moon to full moon. Your machete will be that much stronger of a tool, and you have consecrated your sacred tool for the spirits and future conjures.

This working can be done at any time of the year, so long as you are able to dig a shallow hole in the ground.

The machete can be placed on or near your altar for the U.G.R.R., or it can be positioned near your doorway, as some do. Standing it by a doorway is a way of invoking its protective qualities. At times when we feel that bad juju is possibly at our doorstep, the simple act of holding and feeding the machete and telling it what we want it to do can be enough to ward it off, as well as give us a commanding sense about us. Once we feed and use the machete as a tool for the spirits, it can house protective energy for quite some time, especially if we put that magic toward it. It will act as a ward as well as cut and sever any bad magic that may be coming our way. The machete can also be the tool for Captain John Brown, and so again we can see that the machete is a multipurpose blade for our U.G.R.R. conjuring purposes.

To Wade in the Water: Cleansing and Ritual Baths

To enlist Mama Moses and her Followers in a ritual bath can be beneficial for rejuvenation as well as cleansing or removing binds and blocks.

Bath for Rejuvenation and Recharging

- Light up your altar or the workspace you have created for Mama Moses and her Followers.

- Clean your bathtub of usual items that can accumulate—shampoos, conditioners, soaps, etc.—making it temporarily uncluttered.

- Fill the bath with water at your usual temperature for comfort.

- While it's filling, add a dash of Florida Water or Hoyt's Cologne, as well as a few drops of any essential or "condition oil" you are familiar with or have created for the purpose of rejuvenation. Some examples of an essential or perfumed oil for rejuvenation are lavender, peppermint, and lemon.

- Add some flowers and/or herbs, either purchased or gathered from your local surroundings. These could include roses, common dandelions, or any flower that brings you comfort. Herbs to use could be the commonly found broadleaf plantain that grows in most yards and between concrete cracks in most cities, chamomile in any form—even tea—and ginger in any form.

- Have a jar candle as well as a taper available and ready.

- Once the bath is filled and contains the ingredients mentioned, turn off the light and get ready to begin.

- Light the taper candle from your altar, and then light the jar candle or tea light from it. Place the jar candle/tea light down, preferably in front of you on your tub's surface or shelf so you can see it while bathing.

- Hold on to the taper candle with both hands, focused and ready for your ritual bath.

- Recite:

> *Mama Moses, Mama Moses, Mama Moses,*
> *Come to my side as I wade into the water to cleanse and recharge;*
> *help anoint and rejuvenate me.*

- Step into the bath and sit down, still with the lit taper candle in your hand.

- Sit there for a moment and focus on your taper candle. Know you are submerged in water illuminated by its flame, sanctifying your spirit and surrounding water.

- Call to her again:

Mama Moses, help me cleanse and rejuvenate my mind, body, and soul.

- Extinguish your taper by submerging it in the bathwater and place it off to the side.

- Begin to cup the water in your hands and rub it on your body, down your arms, your torso, your shoulders. Cup and dribble the water all about your body as you recite: "Mama Moses, help cleanse me with your holy light and rejuvenate my spirit."

- Once you are done washing your body and feel that tangible connection, sit back and relax for a bit. Think of the things you want washed away and the things you need rejuvenated in your soul, projects you want to accomplish, tasks you want to achieve. Let those visions sink into your being while the ingredients and presence of spirit rejuvenate you.

- Once you feel your bath and work have been accomplished, thank Mama Moses for her help in cleansing you in the waters you have made sacred:

Mama Moses, I thank you for your aid.
I thank you for anointing me in the cleansing waters.
Mama Moses, I bid you love and Godspeed.

- Cup one more handful of water, dribble it over your head, and then exit the tub.

- Drain your bath, and dry and dress yourself.

- This is a good time to anoint the crown of your head with Jerusalem oil.

- Gather the flowers or herbs you placed in the tub and discard them, preferably outside later that night or the next day. I personally like to scatter them to the outdoors and nature, but as this is a rejuvenation bath as opposed to one of a more serious nature, disposing them in the trash will suffice.

Note: If you do not have a bathtub, then improvisation will be needed. All of the previously mentioned can be mixed into a bucket or large pot of warm water. You will need to enter a candle-lit shower and distribute the concoction by pouring it on yourself in increments and doing your best to emulate the procedure above.

Jerusalem Oil: U.G.R.R. Anointing Oil

For the purposes of an anointing and dressing oil for works among and for the spirits of the U.G.R.R., we can use the oil that has legacy here in Canaan North, at the terminus of Mama Moses's tracks to freedom. "Jerusalem oil" has a history among the descendants of the freedom seekers who put down roots in St. Catharines, and more than one family in particular has carried on the concocting of a blessing and condition oil as it pertains to the mysteries and allegory of the U.G.R.R. If we are using oils for any of the countless reasons one does in rootwork, conjure, and witchcraft, how can we not include the one that is a part of tradition used by the very descendants of freedom seekers who traveled on the freedom train with Mama Moses? This is basic, yet sacred.

The formula may sound simple, but remember that symbolism and what is available were paramount for not only those that traveled the U.G.R.R. but in this case also long after for those that made it across the proverbial River Jordan.

When this was shown to me—the name and the recipe along with a vial used for protecting houses, churches, and one's spirit—is a moment I won't soon forget.

- The base of Jerusalem oil is kosher olive oil imported from Israel. Kosher oil imported from Israel is the most integral foundation according to tradition, but if this is not available, regular imported Israeli olive oil will suffice. Either can be purchased at most Jewish groceries or food supply stores in just about any city in North America.

- You can keep the bottle as your supply for a good amount of time, and you will want to, as it's not exactly cheap, and not uncommon for a few friends to go in on a bottle together. Transfer some to a smaller bottle or preferably a vial as needed. Fill the vial halfway.

- You will then want to get some hyssop oil, available at just about any shop or independent creator that has a good selection of essential or perfumed oils.

- Once you have transferred the olive oil to your vial, fill the other half with hyssop oil.

- Shake the vial well.

Basic, simple, sacred.

I cannot stress enough how precious creating this blend of anointing oil is for anyone who will work among the spirits of the U.G.R.R. This is as sacred and traditional, as well as original, as one can get for a dressing and blessing oil, sourced from the tradition of historic families that still resides across the River Jordan. This can be used to bless and protect your home, your place of worship, or tools and implements you hold dear, not to mention your own body and spirit while anointing your crown. Depending on the purpose Jerusalem oil can be both an anointing and condition oil. It would be a good oil to seal your work when cleansing your Bible, for example.

Anointing Prayer

When we dress, bless, or anoint anyone, ourselves, or tools, this is the prayer that is said:

As the mountains surround Jerusalem, so the Lord surrounds his people, from this time forth and forevermore. —Psalm 125:2

This signifies and affirms that those blessed by the Lord shall not be shaken and stand as strong as Mount Zion. When you say these words, whether to yourself, to another, or while anointing your tools, you are the priest or priestess bestowing the prayer and do so in the name of the spirits of the U.G.R.R.

The same prayer is said with a slight alteration upon mixing and creating the Jerusalem oil blend. Once you have your oil in a vial or container for use, hold it close to your heart, meditate with it, and recite: "General Tubman, empower this Jerusalem oil with protection and blessings from your place in spirit. Just as the mountains surround Jerusalem, so the Lord surrounds his people, from this time forth and forevermore." You can then place the oil on your altar or shrine to further charge. If you were to make enough to fill a small jar, then you can further charge it by placing a candle on the lid to bless and illuminate it with flame. The mystery of the Jerusalem oil is unique, as it carries the allegories of the days of the U.G.R.R. by relying on biblical verses for its ingredients, in particular from Exodus:

- When it comes to an anointing oil: "You shall make of these a holy anointing oil, a perfume mixture, the work of a perfumer; it shall be a holy anointing oil." (Exodus 30:25)

- When it comes to the olive oil: "You shall charge the sons of Israel, that they bring you clear oil of beaten olives for the light, to make a lamp burn continually." (Exodus 27:20)

- When it comes to the hyssop oil: "Cleanse me with hyssop, and I will be clean; wash me, and I will be whiter than snow." (Psalm 51:7)

The above formula is of course pragmatic, basic to a degree—the imported kosher olive oil notwithstanding. Jerusalem oil is for magical purposes, originally meant to be created on a whim or out of necessity when needed. However, should you be a person who enjoys creating oils or enjoys oils with a pleasant or intoxicating aroma, then we can add to this formula to customize, enhance, or personalize it a bit. Doing so is something I have had great discussions over, as well as divined about, and so I assure that there is no disrespect in doing so, so long as the foundations and essential ingredients are adhered to and the historic and sacred nature of Jerusalem oil is understood. If you are inclined to experiment, then I will share my own addition to the Jerusalem oil to demonstrate a way to enhance it if desired.

When it comes to adding fragrance, which could be for the purpose of employing Jerusalem oil for love, sweetening magic, or just to have a pleasant aroma upon you to enhance and remind you of your connection to this spirit world, then here is a way to do so while maintaining the traditions from which it was born.

To the already existing vial of Jerusalem oil I add a few drops of myrrh and cinnamon oil. Both provide a pleasant aroma, as well as a few other elements to be drawn from energywise. While neither myrrh nor cinnamon is part of the original Jerusalem oil, they both figure within the ingredients of the "holy anointing oil" recipe bestowed by God unto Moses as found in Exodus:

> *Take the finest spices: 500 shekels of liquid myrrh, 250 shekels of fragrant cinnamon.—Exodus 30:22*

If you add to the base formula of Jerusalem oil, maybe you will decide to use other ingredients for other purposes from other biblical sources or your own ideas.

The mysteries of the Jerusalem oil, carrying on the cloaked and biblically sourced incantations for the purposes of conjure, are something that I hope as this tradition spreads are carried on, shared, and given the light it deserves among the many other anointing and condition oils used among those who conjure the "root"—the spirit. To me, it's perfection in every way and its mysteries profound. When we use Jerusalem oil, we honor a tradition from the holiest grounds of U.G.R.R. terminus at the end of the very tracks of Harriet "Mama Moses" Tubman. Create it, share it, sell it, Godspeed.

Bath for Removal of Binds, Blocks, and Negativity/Bath for Uncrossing

Unlike the rejuvenation bath, the uncrossing bath is something to do if you feel that you have been "crossed" or hexed by way of a person or persons that view you with less than favorable intentions. Potentially, the very act of envy or jealousy can attach to you and your spirit. This is called the "evil eye" by predominantly Italian, Mediterranean, and certain Middle Eastern and North African cultures, but in the Americas it's often referred to as being "crossed." In a worst-case scenario someone may have taken the time to do actual magic for your being unlucky, confused, or ill, at which point the condition is called being "cursed."

I have always been taught by my teachers to be self-maintaining, self-protected, and to do any number of things before seeking help from another worker or clergy. I subscribe to this, as many underestimate their own ability to recognize and remove that which afflicts them, magically speaking. So if you feel you have been crossed or cursed, then your intuition is already at work, and before you seek help from a person possessing the skill set for such things, I recommend you seek the aid of Mama Moses with one of her strongest attributes: removing binds and blocks. Begin your own practice of self-maintenance with her help. This exercise has had years of success among multiple people, or I would not share it within these pages.

Finally, you should keep in mind that the very act of being in certain company or certain environments can call for something a little more than a bath of rejuvenation. Many people who feel crossed or cursed are suffering from what is best described as an "energetic" flu or cold, which can infect us from numerous situations. Ideally these are something we can "wash away" on our own. You may need to do a little research for some of the herbs and oils, but I have still listed a few examples below. Should you already have knowledge of herbs, oils, and formulas for uncrossing, then maybe including Mama Moses in your formula will be unique. One could choose a few of the items listed here or add them all for one big potent wash.

- As with the rejuvenation bath, light up your altar for Mama Moses and her Followers.

- Clean the tub of clutter as mentioned previously.

- Begin to fill your tub.

- As it fills, add a dash of Florida Water as well as a few drops of any condition or essential oil you are familiar with, have purchased, or have created for the purpose of "uncrossing" or "jinx removal." Some examples of essential oils are cedarwood, frankincense, mint, and rosemary.

- Add any flowers or herbs, preferably ones that are for the purposes of removals and uncrossing. Some options can be found in your very own backyard or the area surrounding your home, growing in concrete or gravel, particularly nettle (pick carefully, but it's very effective), broadleaf plantain, or roses.

- Add one of the commonly found "bluing agents" for laundry—used in many traditions for cleansing. These balls or little blocks are found in most large department stores—popular brands being Mrs. Stewart's Bluing and Reckitt's Crown Blue. Your local botanica may carry them as well as an independent creator. Using bluing water for jinx removal is rooted in the pragmatic means and ways of the African American hoodoo practitioner for its "haint blue" qualities, the color being known to protect from negative energies. The practice eventually spread to other North American traditions of conjure and rootwork, most notably up and down the entire Appalachian mountain range.

- Add a pinch of salt, preferably sea, Himalayan, or kosher.

- Add a handful of Epsom salt.

- Add a teaspoon of white vinegar.

- Add a squirt of holy water, if you subscribe to or believe it would help.

- Squeeze half a cut lemon into the water, then place the lemon half into the water.

- Add one cup of liquid black coffee, either purchased or instant.

- Stir the bath, which is about to become a veritable cauldron for your cleansing.

- Once the bath is filled, light a jar candle or tea light and place it at the front of the tub where you can see it.

- Have a black taper candle ready.

- Turn off the light and begin.

- Call to Mama Moses:

    General Tubman, General Tubman, General Tubman,

    I call to you and your powers of cunning and conjure.

  Mama Moses, I ask from you and your Followers to help remove my binds, remove my shackles, and uncross my spirit.

- Begin to rub down your entire body from head to toe with the black taper candle, letting it absorb the negative energy or jinx that binds you.

- Once you have rubbed down your body, light the black taper candle, and enter the tub and sit down with the taper candle in your hand.

- Recite:

Mama Moses, I ask that you come to my side as I wade into the water. I ask for you and your rootworkers to heal me, uncross my spirit, remove my jinx, sever the binds that hinder me, hide my tracks from those that mean me harm.

- Focus on the black taper candle that has absorbed the malignant energy, and then submerge it under the water, extinguishing it, and leave it in the water.

- Begin to wash and cleanse your body, starting from a dribble upon your head, then down your shoulders and arms. Rub your entire body down while submerged in your cauldron bath.

- While washing and cleansing yourself, recite numerous times: "Heal me, Mama. The water heals."

- Rub yourself down with any of the flowers or herbs you have placed in the bath, letting their energy and quintessence draw out the jinx along with the magical and healing properties of the herbs and oils.

If you know who may have crossed you or at least have a good sense as to what has bound you, this is the time to think of it, and see that curse broken and washed away in your ritual bath blessed by Mama Moses and her Followers.

You are not just doing this uncrossing by yourself; you are being accompanied by Mama Moses and her Followers in one of their most potent cures: the removal of binds.

- Once you are finished with your cleansing and you feel that you have successfully removed that which has crossed you, step out of the bath backward—the opposite of how you came in—and when you are out of the tub, make a cross or "X" motion with your left hand to seal off and close the road to the negativity you washed away.

- Thank Mama Moses:

  Mama Moses, I thank you and your cunning folk for helping remove my binds and uncrossing my spirit. I bid you love and Godspeed.

- Scoop out a cup of the bathwater in a container, and drain the tub. Dry and dress yourself. This is a good time to anoint the crown of your head with Jerusalem oil, reciting the prayer shared with the recipe. Once the tub is drained, gather what ingredients are left there, including the black candle, and dispose of them outside in any way that you can. Cast the container of bathwater to the air in a traditional manner: in the direction toward the setting sun to enlist the "takedown" powers it possesses.

Once these steps are completed and you are dried and dressed, have confidence in your own personal magic and that you have taken the steps to claim your freedom from binds and blocks. This process may need to be repeated a few nights in a row—you will know if this necessary or not. If there is an issue that is very serious hex-wise, then you should consult a professional worker skilled in these matters.

Ritual bathing is a good practice to instill into your routine. You may eventually come to use these elements to help cleanse and uncross others, which is totally fine if you feel it is effective and you are confident with the process. Use your intuition and listen to your spirit as to when it would be beneficial or necessary to "wade in the water" and be cleansed, blessed, and dressed by Mama Moses and her Followers.

As with the rejuvenation bath, if you do not have a bathtub, then you will need to improvise and adapt to create this wash in a large container or pot and administer the formula incorporating a shower.

As we can see, working with the spirits of Mama Moses and her Followers has a set pattern: lighting up her altar to establish the doorway, making offerings when necessary, keeping fresh water available on the shrine, petitioning the spirits with your needs, being in a place of gratitude when working with them, and, of course, adapting your work and conjures with them as your intuition guides you. What I offer is a foundation, a starting point to building a relationship with a holy woman and her surrounding spirits. These are the first steps everyone must take in the conjuration of Harriet "Mama Moses" Tubman.

The Nameless Lovers, St. Catharines, circa 1850s, Rick Bell Family Fonds

The Lovers:
The Bride and Groom

In the court of Followers of Mama Moses are two spirits in particular with a poignant story that are known to manifest. While they may encompass the legacy of several, they always come as a pair. Their story is told in slightly different ways from South Carolina to St. Catharines, but regardless of origin they represent the fate that befell many a freedom seeker fleeing the Deep South. The compassion and love that we who work within this spirit world have for them runs very deep. They are an example of what it is to honor the nameless spirits of the Freedom Seekers. They are the Lovers, the Bride and Groom, and this is their story.

During the days of the U.G.R.R. just shortly before the Civil War, two lovers well past their prime in age were soon to be branded as useless by their master, and their fate unknown. They had been toying with the idea of stealing away like many had before them, but running away to the light of the North Star was a young person's game, and they worried they would not be able to make the trip at their age. As the Civil War loomed, the cruelty was ratcheted up on the plantation, uncertainty was all around, and the flight for freedom seemed their only hope of not only staying together but also staying alive. The two lovers were respected among their fellow enslaved; they had withstood the test of time and managed to be a couple for more years than most. They were the mother and father as well as grandmother and grandfather to more than just their own kin; they were the elders and beloved. They had made a unique choice to not jump the broom as many on the plantation had for years. They never wanted to be married as slaves, and had always wanted to wed as free people, but the rumors of freedom coming to the slaves was not in sight—no armed freedom men came to liberate the enslaved, as many had heard was going to happen. The lovers were aware of an impending flight for freedom coming by some of the young-uns; they not only heard the songs being sung, but as elders, they also knew of the secret going around. They made their case to the young trickster who was sneaking in and out of the plantation with instructions, times, and places. It was not an easy sell; they were slow and old. But the young folk spoke up, begged the trickster to take them along on the night the train was going to leave, and he eventually and reluctantly agreed. The lovers were so excited, as were their kin for them. They talked for days as the moon rose later and later each night, talking about meeting Harriet Tubman. Surely she would find them on the trails; maybe even she would marry them when they got to Canaan North, for she had the charm and was blessed by the almighty himself. They had a fever all right, running in them like it hadn't in years, making them feel all young again.

The night finally came, they said goodbyes to folks they had known their whole lives, said goodbye to crying babies and adults alike. A song called and echoed into the night from the woods; the signal was sung, first one person, then dozens joined in, serenading them as the train rolled out. Their journey to freedom had begun, hallelujah!

No one knows just what the days that turned into weeks were like for the old lovers, except they sure managed to keep up. It was as tough as it could get, trudging through swamp and marsh, up to the waist for days they say those trails were. No one knows what happened, really, except that the woman became critical, whether from sickness, snakebite, or her body just giving out, but one thing was for certain: she wasn't going any farther. The runaways did indeed spend a day longer than they should have, tried everything they could, but to no avail. They couldn't wait any longer, the train had to roll on. The old dear told her man to go on—go be free, she begged him with tears in her eyes—there was no hope for her. He was having none of it—it wasn't going to happen. The others tried reasoning, grabbing at him even; he was having none of it. He was not leaving his love of so many years behind. There were tears all around, even as the others finally left, sobbing louder than birds. The old man made some comfort for himself and his lady as best he could. With barely any dry ground about, he set up so he could lay down right beside her as he had done for all those years before they even went gray. He embraced his love, kissed her over and over again, singing her favorite songs. That was the last thing the runaways heard: the old man singing to the love of his life. Surely he couldn't sing all day and night; it must have gotten quiet at some point. But he never let her go. Their embrace alone in that marsh is how they perished together, and they never let go of each other. They are still in each other's arms, even today. Those old lovers, that's their story: somewhere out in those marshes their bodies are still locked together, but their spirits are free. They never did let go of one another, and they never will.

The Lovers and their legacy are sadly how many a journey for freedom went and ended: freedom seekers perishing alone in a remote swamp or marsh, never making their way to free territories, their bodies out there somewhere unmarked and forgotten. Each time we build a Cairn and Cross we tell their story. They are the example of what it stands for: a grave marker for those spirits of the U.G.R.R. who have none.

The Lovers take on a role similar to the Umbanda spirits Preto Velho and Preta Velha. They may have perished together before making it to freedom, but for those that revere and love them, honor and placate them, they will answer and bring to bear their immense powers of love. And the

Lovers are the spirits that bestow love magic. They are the ones that can gift you with love or protect the love you seek. They are the two spirits that manifest the most. When they arrive, it's always joy and love they carry with them, for they are celebrated to this day—and often married to each other in full devotion by spirit workers. Yes, they can cause an emotional reaction; we can tear up when telling or even reading their story. My eyes get wet most every time I share their legacy. But that's a healthy kind of emotional expression: to shed a tear in the name of love and reverence can be cleansing and good for the soul. And in truth, working with many of these spirits can bring out an emotional response.

Before we ask of the Lovers anything love related, we must first marry them. No matter how many times they have been married by conjurers, witches, and the like, they never tire of it. It feeds them and keeps them surrounded by the love and reverence they deserve. Making these two spirits happy as the Bride and Groom brings such a joy to the heart and soul.

Marriage of the Bride and Groom: A Joyful Service for the Dead

You will need some accoutrements before starting the ceremony.

- Effigies first and foremost must be acquired. You can use statues from botanicas, as mentioned previously—portraying couples or separate male and female figures that speak to you. As well you can use wood or resin African and Caribbean statues, or the common route of using skeletal figurines—bride and groom style—as found in Mexican or Central American shops or during the Halloween season just about anywhere. Any of these are fine, and I have used all of the above over the years. In the Niagara Voodoo Shrine we have two life-size skeletal figures dressed in full bride and groom regalia, and we've brought them to many locations for the marriage many times. Your imagination and creativity are the only limit—just do them and everyone a favor and never use effigies of European people since the lovers were African Americans.

- A small bottle of champagne or sparkling wine. Purchasing small cheap bottles is absolutely fine.

- Flowers of any kind placed in water. Those picked outside are even better.

- Food offerings, favorably small cakes or pastries.

- Decorative or toy rings. It's the sentiment that counts. The Lovers will be happy with whatever you choose, rest assured.

- Two candles (one each for the Bride and Groom). Any color you choose is fine.

- One candle for you to hold, of any color.

- An additional candle for each person in attendance

- Have prepared a copy of the story of the Lovers to recite.

While it's appropriate to do the wedding at any time of year, the season most associated with the dead will serve as our example—that being the Samhain season and Halloween. This is a good time because of the many ceremonies, rituals, and celebrations held among covens, various spiritual traditions, and communities in general. Quite often these gatherings are open to sharing seasonal celebrations with attendees or exploring other mysteries and traditions honoring the dead. While the marriage of the Bride and Groom can be done solo, it's best experienced with more than one person in attendance as well as helping.

The ritual shared here is a North American Voodoo one, which does not violate any other tradition's regimen or mysteries. With it you are honoring a North American legacy and spirit world that stood for justice and freedom and crossed all boundaries religious, racial, and economic. This is work for the spirits of the U.G.R.R. and nothing else.

This ritual can be done indoors or out. If you can have drummers or a drum available, that would be wonderful, as well as having folks prepared or open to dancing to the drums and for the spirits when the time is right. If drumming is not available, then music played in the background is fine. This can be drumming music, spirituals, or anything that has a jovial and sacred spiritual manner.

Preparations

- If the ritual is held at a location other than your home altar, set up the shrine to Mama Moses and her Followers. Try to have as many of the tools and items listed in the altar setup available as you can.

- Be sure to have the effigies of the Lovers up front in the center of the shrine, or on one set up separately for them, with all the accoutrements for them already listed.

- Have one set of offerings already in place, set on the shrine or altar to Mama Moses and her Followers. And have another set of food and drink offerings ready to be presented later, being sure to leave a space where these offerings can be placed by yourself and the attendees.

- The attire for this ceremony is up to you and the attendees. Any normal clothing or other ritual garb is fine.

Begin the Work

- Start with either drums or music playing to set the tone for the celebration.

- Light up the altar to Mama Moses and her Followers.

- Light the two candles for the Bride and Groom, keeping them close to the effigies, either right beside or behind/in front of them.

- With drums or music playing, consecrate and honor the power of the place you are in and the ground you walk upon. If it's indoors, sprinkle Florida Water to cleanse the floor; if outdoors, again sprinkle Florida Water as well as a libation for the ground of water, alcohol, or tobacco.

- When the time seems right, bring the music and revelry to a stop.

- Call forth to Mama Moses:

Mama Moses, Mama Moses, Mama Moses!

General Tubman, we gather to honor you and your Followers, the Freedom Seekers. We gather to honor the Lovers.

We gather here, Nana Tubman, to commemorate the spirits of the Underground Railroad, may you and your Followers be pleased with our devotion.

Praise be Mama Moses!

- Have attendees answer,

Praise be Mama Moses!

- Light a candle, whether jar or taper, hold it in your hand, and recite the story of the Lovers.

Telling the story of the Lovers is a true incantation. This, along with the prior setup and consecration of the sacred space, will bring forth their presence.

When you have finished telling their story, begin to illuminate the candles the attendees are holding. They can be lit off of one another's or a person can go around and light each one—whatever makes most sense for the situation.

Once the candles are lit, have folks assembled near the altar and bring everyone's attention to the effigies.

- Tell everyone present: "We have heard the story of the Lovers who fled for freedom, wishing to be married as free people. We now honor tradition and marry the spirits that were not wed in life."

- Recite:

To the spirits that fled as lovers, longing to be married in freedom,
we bestow you with a wedding in your honor.

- Proceed to the effigies and pick up the rings. Hold them high and recite:

To the Lovers that yearned to be married,
a token and symbol of your eternal love.

- Place the rings upon or at the base of each of the effigies and recite:

May you wedded spirits always be in each other's embrace, tonight and
forever. May you always be surrounded and loved. We who have gathered in
your honor decree it so: you are Bride and Groom!

- Be jubilant, with cheering or applause if possible, drum rolls, etc.

- Recite:

We bid the Bride and Groom to stay with us, share with us,
and let the living and the dead celebrate eternal love together!

This is a good time to begin the music or drumming again. While the music plays, folks can begin to take their candles and place them at the altar nearest the effigies for the Bride and Groom. If you are outdoors, they can be put right upon the ground. Have the attendees bid the Bride and Groom good tidings while doing so, offering them love and blessings.

Begin to present the food offerings that were brought, placing these among the candles at the shrine for their wedding. As always, make the cross motion before doing so.

Once the food offerings have been given, open the bottle of champagne or sparkling wine, hold it high, and toast: "To the Bride and Groom!" Take a small sip and spray it into the air from your mouth toward the effigies. This shares the libation with the spirits and your essence with them.

- Hold the bottle high again and toast: "To the spirits!" Now pour some out onto the ground (or into another glass placed near the altar if you are indoors).

- Pour some more into a glass, hold it high, make the cross motion with it, and place it at the effigies, toasting again: "To the Bride and Groom!"

- Share what's left with the attendees or enjoy a good drink for yourself. The spirits will be happy to share.

Let the celebration continue for a while, as long as you see fit. Focus on the altar as often as you can, and see the shrine all aglow, illuminated with abundance, love, and light. Make this your moment to connect to the spirits yet again. If there are other attendees, this is a good time to go to the altar by yourself and feel its power, soak it in, say your own words to the Bride and Groom you have held this joyful service for. Let their gratitude envelop your spirit, take it all in, and know Mama Moses will be pleased at your devotion and sacrifice to tradition. You have provided a rare gift to sacred spirits. You are blessed.

When the time seems right, gather everyone's attention and thank everyone for coming, bringing offerings, and providing their service for the spirits. If there were drummers or a drummer, this is the time to thank them too.

- Focus everyone's attention on the shrine and altar again, and recite:

Congratulations to the Bride and Groom! Be in each other's arms now and forever. Surrounded by the love of the living, you are free.

You will never be forgotten, and you will always be loved, Godspeed!

- Thank Mama Moses and her Followers:

Nana Tubman, we thank you and your Followers.
We hold this service for you and the spirits you love.

Mama Moses, may your light shine and may you and your Followers be ever loved. Praise be Mama Moses and Godspeed!

- Let your space continue to be lit until you decide to shut it all down.

It's a large task to facilitate the marriage, at least with others in attendance. But this is a ritual that will bring great reward to you and the spirits, as well as anyone else present. It will have a deep and lasting impact upon you, as you have provided a true service for two beautiful and inspiring spirits of the U.G.R.R.

High John the Conqueror: The Prince of Conjure

Few spirits of conjure and rootwork in the Americas exemplify the elements of the practice more than the sacred spirit of High John the Conqueror. In life, High John the Conqueror was royalty, a divine prince of his lineage from the Congo. His noble status did not protect him from the warfare of the times, however. He was kidnapped, imprisoned, sold into slavery, and shipped to the Americas on the Middle Passage. Once there, he demonstrated his unique strength, stubbornness, and unwillingness to be subjugated: He would not be made subhuman. No, he would fight and survive in epic fashion. He never relinquished his power to the torturers, never cooperated with the orders of the "masters." His ancestral bloodline and its deities enabled him to overcome many things. If he was ordered to do a job, he refused. If he was confronted by his enslaver, he outsmarted him. If he was threatened, he showed no fear; if beaten, no pain. Stories of his strength spread among those held in slavery's chains, as he broke and defied every rule. His tales brought comfort and hope, for he persevered through horrendous ordeals set before him and many times did so with humorous anecdotes, which spread like contagion. His unbreakable spirit would become legendary and inspire his fellow captives for generations.

At some point High John fled not only his bondage but his human body, leaving the shackles of slavery and the human condition behind to take his place among the clouds and stars, returning to his ancestral Africa. From his place among the mysteries and glorified ancestors of his people he could do more for those still in bondage than he could have as a human. From spirit he could bless his people and alleviate their suffering, and he left his power in the form of a secret root that could be used to call his spirit forth and enlist his aid. Even the great Frederick Douglass utilized his root while a prisoner to slavery, as well as one of the Conqueror's cousins while fleeing to the Free North. This was his most sacred gift: he could be invoked at the cruelest and harshest moments of the torture and beatings that the enslaved regularly endured to take the soul of a person to a faraway place, removed from their body's pain and joining the ancestors high above the Earth. There are many accounts of this very blessing that survive in slave narratives and interviews with those who endured well past emancipation.

And while there was indeed a concoction that could be consumed prior to expected torture to alleviate the pain, even those that did not have such an aid invoked his very spirit to come and steal them away from torturous pain. There are heartbreaking stories of those who would be whisked away from the whipping pole and in their mind adorned in fine dress and carried away to a place of sunshine and the embrace of those they had loved and lost. This was the work of the Prince of Conjure at his most sacred. While men and women would eventually be returned to the unimaginable pain of their bodies at their torture's end, they were, however, not present during the beatings—free for those moments, their spirit enveloped by the power of High John the Conqueror, the Prince of Conjure.

In the realm of spirit High John continued to outsmart and conquer many—including the Devil himself. High John attracted the eye and fell in love with the Devil's daughter. None too impressed, the Devil gave High

John a series of impossible tasks to overcome. The Devil's daughter helped High John, warning him that the Devil meant to take his soul should he fail. High John and the Devil's daughter rode off on the Devil's own steeds, galloping away to avoid capture, shape-shifting each time the Devil got on their trail. High John outsmarts and conquers the Devil to this very day.

There is no obstacle that the Prince of Conjure cannot help you overcome. He breaks down doors literally and figuratively. Like all the spirits of the U.G.R.R., he will come to your call, but you must truly understand and respect his place and whom he set out to originally serve. A spirit of his nature—able to see time continue to travel like sand in an hourglass—was aware of the U.G.R.R. and those who managed it, aware of the good souls of every color, and blessed his people that chose to steal away as he did and fight for their freedom on secret tracks. Those who made it to Canaan North surmounted many obstacles, trials, and tribulations, and countless travelers had one of the greatest allies on their side in High John the Conqueror.

But like many aspects of modern conjure, voodoo, and rootwork, the legacy and sacred power of High John the Conqueror has been watered down for mainstream consumption and appropriated by some as a curio for gambling, good luck, and sex. This was perhaps made easier because during the era of enslavement, the Prince of Conjure was a highly guarded secret, especially from the enslavers, so much so that to this day his place among the mysteries is unknown by many of the masses who enlist his root's power.

Commercial entities that cater to conjure, hoodoo, and rootwork even depict him as a conquistador or Spanish king, and a pale one at that, on oil and candle labels. While High John and his "cousins" can and will aid a person in those pursuits he is widely known for and may respond regardless of packaging, the disconnect from his legacy is an insult. The Price of Conjure was not only a paramount part in surviving the horrendous treatment that was slavery, but he was a companion on countless journeys to freedom on the U.G.R.R., encouraging and blessing thousands of his people during their flight to the Promised Land.

In spite of these indignities, High John and his magical legacy live on and are attainable though the reciprocity between us humans and his sacred root: *Ipomoea purga,* a plant related to the morning glory and sweet potato. It is known by the common names bindweed and jalap root. We have already seen uses for High John the Conqueror root in this book so far, so here in this section we can learn of his sacred legacy as well as how to empower, feed, bless, and dress this sacred root. When procuring your High John from a botanica or business, be sure that the root is whole, rather than sliced, as some businesses strangely sell. The root's power is most accessible when it is intact. If you are fortunate enough to be able to find the root in nature, you are in a small and admirable group; but be sure to harvest it in a sacred manner, for when we harvest a root of any plant, that is a literal "sacrifice," and the plant's life force as well as the ground it grows from should be honored and thanked from a place of gratitude.

Many scholars feel that another trickster overlaps with the legacy of High John the Conqueror. And that is Brer Rabbit. After all, when Brer Rabbit outsmarted Brer Fox, it was the "master" that was being fooled and mocked. In all truth this is an entirely different spirit, but their stories have been conflated as the secret kept High John and his power hidden. Cloaking the tales of High John in the humor-tinged fables of the trickster Brer Rabbit in tales of walking, talking animals and their childlike anecdotes meant they could be easily brushed off as silly stories by enslavers.

Empowering and Feeding
High John the Conqueror Root

There are several means and formulas to empower and feed a High John the Conqueror root. The method I share here is my favorite and, in fact, a combination of elements of southern, northern, and Appalachian conjure.

- Take your High John root in your hands, and commune with it. Hold it and ponder all that this spirit meant to his people kept in bondage.

- With your left pointer finger, tap the root three times, and whisper aloud: "Awake and remember your power."

- Breathe upon the root, and say his name: "High John, I call you forth."

- Pour a dribble of whiskey into a small container or shot glass, and place the root into this vessel so it can suck up the whiskey and gain its power. Let the root sit in the whiskey for about half an hour or so.

- When you take the root out of the whiskey, handle it for a while as it dries, breathe upon it again, and call on High John again: "High John, fed and full, I honor you."

The root is now empowered, fed, and charged. It has been awoken and is ready for your needs, whether it will be placed in a mojo bag or used to infuse another concoction or simply carried on its own, as we learned in the earlier ritual To Carry Mama Moses upon You, or placed upon an altar among her accoutrements. For a time—at least a moon cycle or two—it will be able to bring forth the blessings needed to overcome obstacles or strengthen your magic. Just be sure to always hold it, rub it, and tell him what you need. It is best to feed and empower the root every few moons at worst, as the stronger the root, the stronger the relationship and magic that will manifest.

The whiskey that is left over from feeding the root is not to be consumed for any reason. You can either offer it to the ground outside at your convenience or keep it in a small lidded container, adding more leftovers after each feeding, and then use it as a dressing concoction for a blessing. This, like fresh whiskey in general, can be used to feed the root once in a while or when you feel compelled to do so. It is entirely up to you.

Another way of empowering your High John root without whiskey is to place the root on a bed of freshly shredded or cut gingerroot. Then cover it up in shredded/cut ginger as well and leave it like that for a day or so before following the formula above. Gingerroot has a potency to it that charges up other roots, giving them strength and vigor. In fact, certain mojo hands will contain a small piece of gingerroot among the other ingredients for the sole purpose of enhancing High John's power.

This seems a good place to define a "mojo hand." Traditionally, a mojo bag was referred to as a "hand." This was because in an era long ago, there were often actual bones from a human hand placed within the mojo itself. The hand or finger bones were sourced from graves and dug up by workers,

---

I would be remiss in not mentioning here as well that gingerroot in and of itself is a potent root for many magical purposes, as well as medicinal. Ginger has its own identity, sacredness, and life force. It too is the heart of a plant, and its potency lasts for a good while. So when and if you enlist the gingerroot, take a moment to honor its life force. There is an entire formulary for utilizing gingerroot—known as jake root in the Caribbean—for conjure and rootwork, as well as with Asian sorcery. I recommend you get to know this root and its spirit, as it is such a beneficial one for everything from good health to love magic and, of course, enhancing High John the Conqueror.

and at times certain types of graves were turned to for certain purposes depending on the need at hand, enabling the fetish to "grab hold" of the magic sought after. It's still a term used among traditional workers.

As we move beyond harvesting and feeding our High John the Conqueror root, note that on a medicinal level, High John is used to overcome stomach ailments and parasites and acts as a potent laxative. So do not consume it! However, we can see how its mundane use parallels its spiritual attributes of overcoming obstacles and clearing paths. When certain businesses sell High John Root sliced and cut, it's most likely for herbal/medicinal practices best left to professionals of that trade. Again, never use cut or sliced root, but only whole intact High John root for magic and conjurations.

Uses for High John the Conqueror

- **To enhance a connection to Mama Moses.** When you want to feel the closeness of Mama Moses, place a fed and empowered root on her altar or shrine. After a while take the root and ask High John, the Prince of Conjure, to bless and keep clear the path between you and the spiritual force of Mama Moses. Carry the root upon you undressed or wrapped in a small cloth and know that you are connected to Mama Moses and her shrine as well as blessed by the presence of the Prince of Conjure. Mama Moses herself carried the Prince of Conjure with her on many of her secret journeys.

- **For strengthening your divination work.** To enhance your divination or to bless your work with the Diviners, keep a fed and empowered root upon you or beside the candle or effigy of the Diviners you wish to work with. This will enable a stronger and better connection to their blessings and manifestation for you when working or enhancing your craft.

- **To amplify love magic.** As the Prince of Conjure does bestow sexual blessings as well as enhance love magic, it's good to place a fed and empowered root upon any shrine or beside any effigy for the Lovers. When we have already made the connection to the Lovers themselves, the Prince of Conjure can only make it much more potent, as well as accompany the Lovers and grace them with fraternity among spirits. When we enlist the magic of the Lovers, any magic created with them is best done with the Prince of Conjure's root as well as his friend the jake root, aka ginger. We can carry High John root when we go looking for love, sex, or to enhance our lovemaking. This goes for both men and women.

- **To magnify healing magic.** As with the Diviners and Lovers, the Healers and their holy conjures can be boosted with the aid of High John the Conqueror. When we enlist the Healers, a fed and empowered root can be placed on the altar to be charged by the holy work and given to a loved one or colleague to carry to work to cure their tribulations. We can carry the charged root ourselves to enhance and extend the work we need or ask for. The Prince of Conjure, a conqueror of all obstacles on a blockbuster level, can only make our healing magics that much more effective. Place the root for the Healers upon the Bible you keep on the altar to honor and work with them.

- **To help you overcome obstacles.** In everyday life we all need to overcome many things at home, at work, and in our family dynamics at times. Take a fed and empowered root and carry it on you, either undressed or wrapped in a cloth. Ask the Prince of Conjure for his strength and powers of perseverance, and he will help you overcome the tribulations you face. No matter what challenge we face, he will only work to make it that much easier to endure or overcome.

These are just a few of the ways we can enlist the powerful and sacred mystery that is High John, the Prince of Conjure, via his root and legacy. Once we have empowered his root, the possibilities for him to enhance our work are truly countless. You will undoubtedly come up with ideas of your own or be inspired by his spirit to improvise many applications for his presence, blessings, and magic. By never forgetting his true legacy and whom he truly set out to serve, you will experience a unique and powerful connection to a spirit synonymous with the U.G.R.R. and its secret magic. But before you start experimenting on your own, let's look at an original and powerful mojo for connecting to High John and legacy with the U.G.R.R.: the Mojo Hand of Freedom.

The Mojo Hand of Freedom

The mojo hand of freedom is a type of gris-gris that is meant to connect one to the spirits of the U.G.R.R. and all the freedom they stand for. This mojo will enable one to overcome bindings, shackles, and obstacles, as well as avoid having any laid in front of you in the first place. It honors High John for his position among the mysteries and spirits of the U.G.R.R. as well as the power that Mama Moses has to help us attain freedom and remain free on many levels.

This mojo hand formula was created when my friend the renowned conjurer Orion Foxwood was visiting my home. He and some colleagues were making a pilgrimage of sorts along the legendary route of the U.G.R.R., from Delaware to St. Catharines. The final goal of the trip was for us to facilitate a retreat to honor Mama Moses and the spirits of the U.G.R.R. This may seem like a basic formula to some—and rather nontraditional as well. Some elements of the formula come directly from Orion Foxwood and the Appalachian conjure he works with and teaches.

- A square piece of cloth about four to six inches square. Preferably for this recipe use material from a plaid work shirt; one that has been worn is even better. Any color is good. According to Appalachian conjure, a work shirt has "hard work" and prosperity mana within it. The interceding lines of a plaid patter work to "cross" and protect not only your mojo, but also your spirit in general.

- High John the Conqueror root. This should be of a slightly larger size if possible and fed and empowered before you start the ceremony to birth your mojo hand.

- A buckeye, aka chestnut. While these are seasonal, if you can find one for this mojo that would be great. They do tend to lay beneath the trees intact for quite a while. (You only need the nut, not the formidable casing, although those are good to have sitting on a window ledge or above a door in the house for protection.) The buckeye is for protection and seeing into the other world with the magic of a "buck's eye," which is what the nut resembles. They also represent prosperity and all-around good luck when carried in one's pocket. Many a traveler carried a buckeye on their journey on the U.G.R.R.

- Three small pebbles and about a teaspoon-size mound of earth. Getting these ingredients could be a bit of a challenge or require an excursion, but it will be well worth it in the end. The pebbles and earth should be from a location synonymous with the U.G.R.R. or any of its historic figures—whether a trail, historic house, statuary, cemetery, or plaque. Bear in mind that nearly every part of the North American continent does have something to this effect. If there is not a place of that nature nearby, maybe there is one close to where a friend, family member, or colleague lives, and they could possibly send you some. If you cannot gather these ingredients by such means, then reach out to me via my contact info and maybe I can help.

- Three matches

- An eight-inch length of string. This should preferably be twine, but any kind will do as long as it's not too thick. Any color will suffice.

- A small amount of whiskey

- River, ocean, lake, swamp or rain water. Any living water will be good.

- A candle of any kind. You may use one already charged or one you dedicate for the purpose of this working.

- Jerusalem oil (see p. 72.)

BIRTHING THE MOJO HAND OF FREEDOM

- Once you've amassed your materials and ingredients, lay them all out in front of you.

- Light your candle. It will add the power of flame as well as illuminate your work for the spirits of the U.G.R.R.

- Take the earth in your hand for a short while, and employ the method we already know of breathing on it and asking it to awaken and remember its power. Then lay it out on the plaid cloth in a small mound.

- Take the pebbles and do the same to awaken and empower them. Then place them in the earth.

- Take the buckeye, awaken and empower it, and add it to the pile.

- Finally, reaffirm the awakening and empowerment of the High John root, and place it into the mound of ingredients.

- Take the living water, place your pointer finger into it, stir clockwise as you ask it to awaken and remember its power, and then sprinkle a few drops upon the mound of ingredients, anointing it with sacred water.

- Gather up all four corners of the material and close it off at the top, pinching and fully encircling, being sure the material is tightly wrapped around the ingredients and all the ingredients are tightly bound within the material.

- Strike the three matches one at a time, placing the lit match head into the "mouth" of the mojo—where the material is bound up—by inserting each match quickly into the mouth, which will extinguish it.

- Tie the package closed, nice and tightly with the string, fully binding together all the ingredients. As you are tying the mojo hand closed, with each wrap and knot you make, focus on the power you have conjured forth into the mojo hand and "container" it represents.

- If appropriate, take a small sip of whiskey into your mouth, and spray the mojo bag with it. This is how a traditional mojo bag is fed. By spraying the liquid from your mouth, you are sharing your essence with this "living" hand you have birthed.

- Anoint and bless your mojo hand with Jerusalem oil.

- Hold your mojo hand toward the heavens and recite: "I birth this mojo hand of freedom for the glory of Mama Moses and the spirits of the U.G.R.R. Spirits. Bless this mojo hand, and may I never be bound and always be free. Praise be!"

- Optional: This mojo hand can also be used or another one created to remove a bind or curse on someone else. Feed the hand, and rub the person down with it, letting your mojo take away their issue. Afterward feed the mojo hand and thank it.

Dixie John: The Love Doctor

Dixie John, also known as Low John, is a plant cousin of High John the Conqueror. While not boasting the storied legacy of the Prince of Conjure, Dixie John does have his own personality. Dixie John was a healer, a root doctor, and a bit of a gambler. His unique powers channel through his root into helping marriages persevere over issues of stagnancy and lack of passion. Dixie John's penchant for love and sex magic is one of his most popular attributes to many. He is also invoked for good luck in all forms.

Trillium grandiflorum, also called in certain regions the wake-robin plant and part of the lily family, provides the Dixie John root. The trillium is a spring-flowering plant, hence its folk connection to the robin and love. Trillium plants are hard to identify unless it is spring when their flowers are prominent, so Dixie John's powers are harvested during the season of growth, love, and lust. Harvesting Dixie John in the wild can be an issue depending on where you live. The trillium is considered an endangered plant in many regions, as they like to grow in particular forested areas that are sadly succumbing to urban sprawl and development. In Ontario where I live, the trillium is the official flower of the province and illegal to pick or dig up in the wild. So if you are one who is an avid herb and root gatherer, do so with caution or at least a good "keep six" approach to make sure nobody is watching you do it.

If you are going to harvest Dixie John from nature, which is far more common to the average person than harvesting High John, then it's good to follow a procedure for doing so.

- Commune with and honor the plant, whose life you are about to sacrifice.

- Dig up the plant, giving yourself a few inches of perimeter space around the stem.

- Replenish the hole with whiskey and recover it.

When it comes to trillium, you can take the flower home and store it in water. Place this on any altar or working space you have for the U.G.R.R. spirits or beside your bed for it to share the obvious love magic. To get the most out of this rare plant, milking its quintessence by getting as much out of every part of the plant as you can is a good practice. When its time as a decorative flower seems to be almost done and its life force drained, use it in a ritual bath or dry the flower for love magic applications.

Dixie John is fortunately available to purchase at some botanicas, occult and witchcraft shops, and herbal stores. Use the same formula as we did with his big cousin to awaken the root's power.

- Tap the root to announce your intention to awaken his power.

- Breathe upon the root to offer it life's breath.

- Place the Dixie John into some shredded or cut slices of gingerroot for an hour or so to recharge and nourish the root's power.

Uses for Dixie John

During the era of the U.G.R.R., Dixie John root was used for both his medicinal and magical properties. The root doctor Dixie John, like his big cousin, does have medicinal properties. Some herbalists use his root to aid in childbirth as well as to alleviate menstrual cramps. For these applications he may be found under the names of Birth or Beth root. It is best not to ingest Dixie John root, but to leave that to the professionals. When it comes to potent and popular conjures, however, he is the proverbial Love Doctor. Because of his attributes for boosting love and sex, he is a great companion for the Lovers. Here are some ways to incorporate the Love Doctor into your life.

FOR LOVE AND SEX

- Place the fed root into a small muslin bag and put this into a load of laundry for your bedsheets. You'll have incredible sex on them till your next load. The root's power is essentially spent after one laundry load, and it's best to offer it to the outdoors after that.

- Take the small hairs from the root and sprinkle these about your bed. This too will enhance sexual passions and activity.

- You can take a fed root and put it underneath your mattress, or get two and place one on each side of the bed, one for you and one for you partner.

- If you and your partner are both aware of the need for a recharge in the sex and passion department, then both of you can carry a fed root on your person, asking Dixie John to bless you both with passionate sexual prowess. When you do come together to share your bodies, you will both be a force to be reckoned with.

Chewin' John

Chewin' John, also known as Little John, is the second in High John's family of roots. His powers are held within the *Alpinia galangal*, a member of the ginger plant family. While most associate his magic with aid in court cases and legal issues these days, his is also a far more complex spirit. Chewin' John is able to bestow courage, endurance, strength, heightened psychic senses, good luck, and, like his cousin the Love Doctor, love magic. As a member of the ginger family, his root is also able to assist with stomach issues, including hunger pains. These are the reasons why Little John was a sought-after and welcome guest on many flights to freedom.

While High John and Dixie John are both used on a medicinal level and for our purposes it's best not to ingest them, Chewin' John is safe to ingest. While carrying him on you is beneficial, his powers are best accessed by literally chewing the roots. It may sound overly simplistic, but just that very act of chewing Little John can be magic in and of itself.

It can have an effect upon your spirit as well as bringing you closer to his three Johns cousins.

If you want to harvest fresh Chewin' John, you will have to buy the seeds and cultivate your own plants. But his root is mass-farmed, produced worldwide, and easily available in predominantly Asian food and herb supply stores, as galangal is a popular spice in many Asian culinary traditions. You will also find it in botanicas catering to conjure, as well as curio businesses and herbal stores.

Uses for Chewin' John

During the era of the U.G.R.R., Chewin' John root was most often utilized by freedom seekers for his medicinal attributes: chewing on the root gave them stamina and settled the stomach—helpful on the fraught journey north. But his good luck was also invoked. Bear in mind that not all three or even two of these plant cousins might be readily available to every person needing them. However, the attributes of each could be invoked and called forth from whichever of the cousins was available out of necessity. That confusion of attributes has lasted to this day, puzzling folks not familiar with the intricacies and legacies of hoodoo, conjure, and rootwork.

Nevertheless, to this day Chewin' John's powers toward justice, born on the trails and tracks of freedom, are his most enduring—as well as his penchant for love magic. Because of his influence in love, he is of course another great companion for the Lovers.

The experience of chewing this root varies from person to person, and it can be a very personal one too. Remember it is safe to swallow his juices. The simple and sacred act of preparing and conjuring Chewin' John, which to be honest is not as common as one would think, can manifest many visions and emotions. You can do this to enhance your psychic or divination skills to empower your spirit to see danger ahead as well as reveal obstacles you may not have noticed before that surround you. One beneficial vision—although to some I know well it can be an emotional one—is to catch a glimpse of what some of the spirits of the U.G.R.R. went through on their journey or to have the spirits bestow upon you a formula or magic previously unknown to you. For some descendants of freedom seekers, the act of chewing his root brings an extra connection for ancestral work of knowing what they went through to fight for their freedom. Chewin' John can be an enhancer, as descendants have expressed to me, of communication, but these folks have also pointed out that at times they do not need to enlist roots to catch visions or emotions regarding slavery's horrendous past—that very power and all that comes with it is contained within their very body's blood and spirit.

I spend a lot of time here on Chewin' John: to many the least known or worked of the cousins shy of legal issues. But because we are consuming him and his juice and because we conjure him from his door for the purposes of working with the U.G.R.R. spirit world and his place among it, this act of literally chewing roots can be a potent one and reveal many things.

You will most likely be purchasing Chewin' John. So be sure to empower his root: feeding it and awakening its power.

Empowering Chewin' John

FOR CARRYING CHEWIN' JOHN ON YOU

Use the same formula of tapping, breathing onto the root, and invoking his power.

- Place your roots in a small container with shredded gingerroot as described previously, to enhance and invigorate his spirit through the root's door.

- You can carry a small amount of his fed roots wrapped in cloth or just in your pocket or used in other places you feel his blessings would be welcomed.

He can be placed on the altar with the Lovers along with his cousins, as well as to help enhance work with the Diviners.

FOR COMMUNING THROUGH CHEWING

This is a simple and potent way to fully interact with the powers hidden within the Chewin' John root. Go through this simple rite of preparing his root for chewing.

Your Chewin' John will most likely come in small fragments, depending on where you purchase it.

- Take a few pieces of Chewin' John and place them in a small pot, along with a small amount of water and a dash of sugar. Bring this to a boil, and after a few short minutes at boiling, turn off the burner and let the mixture cool.

- Empty the roots and sugar water into a container. Cover the container with a lid and pray over it for the purposes you need. You can also place a small candle of any sort on top of the lid to enhance and illuminate your work.

- Let the container sit overnight.

- The next day your roots will be ready.

Chewin' John for Court and Legal Issues

- Prepare your Chewin' John roots in sugar water as for communing through chewing.

- Place the roots and syrup water into a container, cover this with a lid, and place a candle on top.

- Pray for the outcome you wish to see come to fruition.

- The next day, take your conjured and prepared Chewin' John and place it in your mouth when the working begins.

- If you are working for an outcome in court, when you enter the room have the root at the ready in your mouth. When the judge comes in, discreetly spit out a small amount onto the floor. This is a good time when folks are asked to rise and there is rustling and adjustment as everyone prepares to stand.

- Now your Chewin' John can work in the court space toward the outcome you deserve and/or desire.

Also, if there is a just cause you want to work in your favor, you can apply another method by writing out on a piece of paper the outcome of a situation that you want to arrive in your favor, especially situations about or including people regarding a legal matter—which could encompass many issues. Take a small mason jar, and place in the jar either your fully written out notes of what you want to achieve or potentially the names of the persons you wish to see work in your favor or even be dominated to serve in your favor (use discretion for that). Then a photo can also be put into the jar along with the written words you have crafted. Then you take your ready for chewin' roots—having previously told Chewin' John of this work and purpose—and begin to chew and then spit the juice and fragments into the jar on top of the words, names, and/or photos that may have been included. By doing this you are spitting your intention onto the outcome you want—sort of bringing court to you, if you will, with Chewin' John as your counsel. Once you have finished chewing and spitting your intention into the jar and contents, close the jar with its lid, seal it with melted wax, and place a candle on top of the jar lid to further empower and illuminate the container magic you have just conjured. It's best to house the jar in a safe and private place. You can continue to charge it as often as you see fit with a candle on the lid. If and when the outcome works in your favor,

open the jar and scatter the contents to nature, and of course, thank Chewin'
John profusely for coming through in your aid.

The Three Johns Together

Our discussion in this chapter should give you a good idea of the vast
number of uses, magics, and blessings that High John, Dixie John, and
Chewin' John can bestow. Still, there is truly nothing like all three combined into one powerful mojo. The formula for combining the Three Johns
into one mojo is common to many, and there are several recipes out there
that enlist them. However, the concept was birthed for the purposes of
traveling on the U.G.R.R.

Most times nowadays a mojo wielded by the Three Johns is in the form
of a Jack Ball—wrapped in a ball and hung from a string, most often used
for gaining luck in gambling. It was also once very common for men to
use the Three Johns Jack Ball to attract women. There is no doubt that it's
a very effective mojo for those purposes, as I can testify. But for a purpose
specific to the U.G.R.R., one that enlisted all the most potent powers this
family of roots could bestow, there is the mojo called The Hand of the
Three Wise Men.

The Hand of the Three Wise Men

With the Mojo Hand of Freedom, we saw a modern recipe to enlist the
blessings of High John along with Mama Moses to help us overcome bindings and obstacles, and also an empowering healing fetish. The Hand of the
Three Wise Men—so named for the Three Wise Men of the Bible—is, on
the other hand, a recipe sourced from the trails and tracks of freedom. While
the Hand of the Three Wise Men invokes much of the same, it's a mojo to
fully envelop one's spirit with the family of roots for a formidable concoction.

Very few freedom seekers were able to flee with enough provisions to
last a few days or the tools to aid in procuring food, let alone clothing to

properly deal with some of the conditions they would endure should they succeed for a month or more. Fewer still were fortunate enough to possess and enlist the Three Wise Men, but some did. This mojo hand will enable you to invoke the entire family of roots. As we have come to see, the blessings from each of them alone can be powerful enough: removing obstacles, breaking down doors, and procuring love, luck, lust, and swagger—in addition to the pragmatic healing powers to aid with cramps, battle various ailments, settle hungry stomachs, and help sustain a person's energy. If a freedom seeker were able to create this mojo hand or given one along the way, they were fortunate, and many swore by its charm to get them by all manner of challenges ranging from rendering them invisible to those that sought to recapture them to helping them avoid traps, staving off sickness, as well as being a focus for prayer, which at times was the greatest aid to a freedom seeker, shoring up their faith and will.

What we will see here is a recipe combining the hand's original formula specifically for travel on the U.G.R.R. and the elements added many years after the fact where the legacy survived. Considering how hard all three Johns were to procure, you will most likely be able to see what was added long after the tracks of freedom ceased to be used.

This work calls for graveyard dirt. This was used to hide a person's tracks on the trails of freedom, making them virtually invisible. Bear in mind that for many who created this hand before fleeing, gathering dirt from a grave plot meant from the one that housed their own ancestors or at the very least their fellow brothers and sisters in bondage. So there was a profound connection in the dirt. Who better to aid them in their flight for freedom than those who sadly had perished while prisoners to slavery? This just goes to show that any African American can arrive at any black burial point, black cemetery, or simply their own family's graves and enlist their blessings for many a historic work with a connection that is simply more sacred or profound than what can be achieved by those of any other ethnicity. This is not to say others cannot make this hand and receive its potent power, but I think some of the other ethnicities forget that while some of this work is intriguing to them, it is the literal blood, sweat, and tears of the African American you are working amid.

INGREDIENTS AND MATERIALS

- High John the Conqueror root, fed and awakened

- Dixie John roots, fed and awakened

- Chewin' John roots, fed and awakened

- Small square piece of cloth of any color. This will be used to wrap up the mojo.

- Graveyard dirt

- Yarn or string to tie off the mojo

- Three matches

- Water gathered from any river, stream, or brook. You will need just enough to sprinkle with.

- Frankincense, either resin, powdered, or a snapped-off piece of an incense stick

- Myrrh, either a piece of resin or a snapped-off piece of an incense stick

- A speck of gold. This can be either a small fragment of gold from an old piece of jewelry or a small purchased piece, or even flakes from any liquor that has it inside as well as a fragment of gold leaf from an art supply shop. Optionally, it can be any form of imitation gold if none of the above can be procured.

- Jerusalem oil (see p. 72).

- A candle. Any color will do.

PREPARING THE HAND OF THE THREE WISE MEN

- Lay out the ingredients for the Hand of the Three Wise Men in front of you.

- Light a candle for your working to illuminate your space and your soul, and to guide the spirits to you, as well as the three biblical Magi themselves. Optionally, have your Bible on hand, and recite from the book of Micah 5:2:

> *But you, Bethlehem, in the land of Judah,*
> *are by no means least among the rulers of Judah;*
> *for out of you will come a ruler*
> *who will be the shepherd of my people Israel.*

- Continue reciting:

> *I call upon the Magi, the Three Wise Men; the astrologer,*
> *the magician, and the diviner.*

> *I call upon the Three Wise Men, for "When they saw the star,*
> *they were overjoyed."*

> *I call upon the Three Wise Men, they who "having been warned in a dream,*
> *not to return to Herod, they withdrew to their country by another route.*
> *When they had gone an angel of the Lord appeared to Joseph in a dream.*
> *'Get up!' he said. 'Take the Child and His mother and flee to Israel!'"*

> *I praise thee wise Magi, and ask that thou bless this hand.*

- Lay your blessed grave dirt in the cloth, in an even circle, reciting:

> *Blessed is the earth my ancestors sleep amongst,*
> *let my pursuers be blind to the routes I travel.*

- Place your fed and awakened High John Root into the grave dirt, reciting:

High John, the Prince of Conjure, be ever wise in my aid and call, help me to conqueror all traps and overpower all obstacles set before me.

- Place three Dixie John roots around the High John, reciting:

Dixie John the doctor, be ever wise in my aid and call, give me the luck to avoid all the snares of thine enemies.

- Place three Chewin' John roots around the High and Dixie John, reciting:

Chewin' John, be ever wise in my aid and call, give me the courage and strength to endure the ordeals set by my persecutors.

- Place your fragment of gold in the mound of ingredients, reciting:

I offer this gold for the king of kings, may I always prosper.

- Place or sprinkle the frankincense on top of the roots, reciting:

I offer this frankincense for the glory of God, may I always be blessed.

- Place your myrrh resin or incense on the mound, reciting:

I offer this myrrh for the rites of thine death, whilst my soul be embraced by the angels.

- Sprinkle a dash of the water on the mound, reciting:

I anoint thee and praise the waters of River Jordan; may many rivers be crossed with ease.

- Gather up the corners of the material and pinch them nice and tight.

- Strike three matches one at a time, and penetrate the opening of the fold as done for the Hand of Freedom.

- Tie off the mouth nice and tight with the string.

- Anoint the mojo with Jerusalem oil, reciting:

  As the mountains surround Jerusalem, so the Lord surrounds his people, from this time forth and forevermore.

- Breathe upon your mojo and then run it over the candle flame quickly, three times, reciting:

  I baptize you with the Holy Spirit and with fire.

- To finish off, recite:

  May I be guided by the holy star unto my Promised Land.

Take a moment or two to hold this mojo close to you, feeling the force you have conjured forth. You have conjured, wielded, and manifested a sacred mojo hand, one blessed by earth, fire, air, and water. You have prayed to and awoken the family of roots in the three Johns, prayed to and invoked the astrologer, magician, and diviner in the Three Magi. This mojo hand will connect you to the magic of the earth, the stars, the prophets and spirits of the U.G.R.R., and you will be blessed by magic of the Three Wise Men—invisible to your enemies, able to overcome all obstacles, earning and achieving the luck you deserve or invoke. A most potent mojo hand is this, may it serve you well.

The Cairn and Cross

The Cairn and Cross: A Monument for the Spirits of the U.G.R.R.

The BME Church in St. Catharines once housed their dead on a plot of land now owned by the Region. When St. Catharines created a city cemetery in the mid-1800s, they went around to all the in-town churches and asked that everyone exhume their dead to be moved to the new cemetery to free up land for the city to expand. Folks did the best they could. But it was known that a few bodies were left behind since, as we've discussed, many of the graves of freedom seekers were quite humble and unable to stand the trials of time. This was true not only for the BME Church, but also the Zion Baptist Church just up the road, where eventually the original church was also demolished and relocated a few blocks away. (Incidentally, this is not just an issue for U.G.R.R. descendants but for many other churches within a few blocks' radius: old Catholic, Anglican, Methodist, Presbyterian, Baptist, and First Nations burial grounds are all extremely close together, and at times bodies reveal themselves below a city street, parking lot, or backyard.)

When I really began to hear and feel the U.G.R.R. spirits share their desires, it was a grave marker for those who had none they presented to me—a charge, if you will. This would be a unique series of works to gain those spirits' trust and begin a dialogue—made a bit easier considering I lived just a few hundred feet from the grounds. Our interactions were both on-site and in my home, where they were welcomed and encouraged to visit. The Cairn and Cross would be my first testament of devotion, the first monument of a type now scattered about North America for honoring the forgotten spirits of the U.G.R.R. that rest in unmarked graves. The Cairn and Cross would not only become a monument and an altar, but the doorway to the entire U.G.R.R. spirit world. Shortly after I erected that first Cairn and Cross, the same spirits presented me with the conjure symbol with all its symbolism, mysteries, and conjuration aspects.

About a year later an older gentleman, a then prominent member—now deceased—of the BME church congregation, knocked on my door and asked if he could come in and look at the shrines. At this point I had begun to attend the occasional service and celebration at the BME Church so that I could spend time behind the walls where Mama Moses prayed and planned during her time in St. Catharines. With my open-door policy and the drumming that frequently rang out from my home, it must have been pretty clear who was erecting crosses out on the city-owned plot behind the church, at least now in hindsight. A little while into the conversation he asked about the symbolism of the Cairn and Cross, which was all about my house in various ways then as it is now. After I told him, he explained to me that, like most of the BME parishioners, he was a descendant of freedom seekers—and not only was this an actual grave marker (used upon those grounds at one time), but also after the bodies were moved, some descendants took the rocks home and have passed them down through family ever since, with his family being one of them. He said I was certainly on the right track and doing the right thing in honoring those who lay unmarked. He was also the third member from the congregation to tell me face-to-face in private that I should not ever talk about any sort of voodoo, conjure, or rootwork while among the BME parishioners. I was fine with that, and even among descendants that are not churchgoers, it's best not to be talking voodoo unless someone brings it up. Even if the flocks in St. Catharines and Chatham are tinged with conjure, as one local descendant told me, because "the 'man' could never beat the African all the way out of us," places like the BME or Zion Baptist Church are houses of God, not temples exalting spirits, so please consider and respect this should you ever visit their churches or communities.

Since then, I have been gifted with one of those very rocks that sat upon a grave as part of a humble cairn and cross. It marked the resting place of a brave soul who walked on foot from Virginia, stopping in Elmira, New York, with John W. Jones, and then joined the train of Mama Moses unto St. Catharines. This is, of course, a very sacred possession and one that I cherish and am blessed to be a keeper of. It sits among other U.G.R.R. antiquities.

So wherever we are, when we create the Cairn and Cross to honor the spirits of the U.G.R.R., we are doing something sacred, something blessed, and something that the very spirits of the U.G.R.R. from Canaan North had asked for. That is the profound symbolism of the Cairn and Cross, what it represents, and the sanctity it invokes. Over the years it has been adopted and claimed by many freedom seeker descendants, and they are in homes, altars, and graveyards across North America built and drawn by people of all colors and all faiths. We do this to enable the work that still needs to be done.

Building the Cairn and Cross

To erect a physical Cairn and Cross is a truly powerful and sacred voodoo that will not only bring a visit from the spirits, but act as a beacon to those that wander. From the elevated to the forgotten, they will recognize it, and they will come. When we build a Cairn and Cross, we show the spirits our devotion to their realm, as well as the love we have for them.

This is a work that can be done on any scale indoors or out, as solitary magic or with a group of people. The rudiments are the same regardless. So as I explain the process and what it means, I am going to do so as I have done for some of the other rituals in this book: as a group activity people can facilitate at any open celebration or festivity at any time of the year. By encouraging groups to explore and experiment with this tradition, it opens the doors for even more to accept or take parts of this tradition as one they are comfortable with and can claim as theirs. Creation of a Cairn and Cross is as original as it gets specific to the U.G.R.R. spirits, and no one can say that it violates or even resembles any other traditions. Quite simply, as we work with the many aspects of this book, it's the intention that you will adopt and contribute to this tradition as it continues to unfold.

There are numerous Cairn and Cross monuments across the continent of North America, and these constitute a grid of magic that connects like tributaries to one another and in turn to the actual tracks of freedom that still run in spirit. The Cairn and Cross will link our conjures together wherever we are like arteries for a sacred river of blood. Some will be permanent; others will only stand for a short while. I have found after seventeen years of erecting various monuments at certain locations that it's best to not get too defeated if one is taken down or vandalized—it happens. The moment that we are building one and the sacred purpose it represents are what is truly magical. I have returned to certain locations to rebuild time and again, albeit with a little less fanfare for those ones, and in truth no matter how decorative, ornate, or impressive we can make them, trust even the humblest will do and be accepted. It is also not an issue if a group of folks build one at a festival or open ceremony setting and then take it down afterward, because it's what happens as we erect one that counts.

Materials for Creating a Cairn and Cross in an Outdoor Setting

- An area that is suitable for however many folks will be present. This can be a forested area, an open field, or a backyard. There really is no spot that is not acceptable. As I'll explain later, even a paved-over area is fine.

- Rocks. How many rocks and how large they need to be will depend on the size of the monument you want to create. You can use any rocks available, including broken pieces of concrete or cinder blocks—we use what we can. For an outdoor setting with several guests or attendees, I have found that a Cairn and Cross that stands about four to five feet tall is best.

- Shovel. If you will be working on earthen ground, a shovel is good for a little predig of a hole to help solidify the eventual cross.

- Wood. What you need will depend on how you decide to make the monument. I have been part of creating crosses out of lashed-together tree branches as well as with two-by-fours, parts of fence posting, and pretty much whatever I can scavenge or have been gifted with over the years. The ideal material would be flat wood that can be either screwed or nailed together, potentially even chiseled out in the center for a flat surface all around. That's of course dependent on talent and tools. I have benefited greatly from many around me who are far better at cross making than I am, and most have been team or community-created; it's all up to you. A flat surface is best to inscribe upon.

- Black magic marker. This could also be paint, but a good thick Sharpie or two is what has been the constant over the years for even the most sacred ones for a permanent structure.

- Candles, any color. For this work—and hopefully the weather will cooperate—it's best to use smaller taper candles, meaning ones that will burn about an hour but not too big. Smaller tapers are ideal, but again adaptability is key. You will need one for every attendee plus three more. I can say that in all my years erecting Cairn and Cross monuments at public rituals in two countries, never has the wind been so extreme as to extinguish the candles. That being said, there was one time in Michigan when we had to move the temporary Cairn and Cross indoors to a large barn because of the wind, and another time in Louisiana we simply used tea light candles inside of clear plastic cups. Adaptability is good in any way we can invoke it.

- The story of the Lovers. Reading or telling the story of the Lovers is a wonderful way to connect to what the Cairn and Cross represents. For some of you that are ambitious and like a big working, a totally wonderful thing to do is both the Cairn and Cross building and the Marriage of the Lovers. These have been combined many times. But at the very least have a copy of the Lovers' story on hand to share.

- Potentially an image of Mama Moses or any of the other historic figures associated with the U.G.R.R. This can help folks connect to their realm. I usually set them off to the side or at a separate altar.

- An image of the Cairn and Cross sigil. It's good to have one on display so we can see the sigil of the altar and doorway we are about to consecrate. This goes well with a photo of Mama Moses at an adjacent altar or set on the ground near the Cairn and Cross.

You can decide to do the construction one of two ways: Predig a hole and place the cross in it, having assembled the rocks up at least a couple of feet high ahead of time, or create it all at once depending on who is in attendance and how you want to present it. It's totally up to you. However, the cross itself is best put together ahead of time.

When it comes to adorning the cross, if the surface can accommodate a marker or paint, it would be ideal to mark the center of the cross with the letters "U.G.R.R." to signify the spirit world we are about to honor. If artistry or talent is afoot, then it is even better to add an image of Ras the Freedom Seeker to the top section of the vertical beam. I have had to enlist many an artist in my time for this over the years, as my skills in that department are severely lacking. You can also adorn the cross in any other way you see fit, whether with quilt codes, a Star of David, or the square and compass. The "U.G.R.R." is the baseline available to just about anybody.

With your rocks and cross at the ready, you may begin to construct your Cairn and Cross.

Erecting the Cairn and Cross Monument

- Start with a prayer of intent:

We gather to erect this Cairn and Cross to honor the spirits of the U.G.R.R. May we be blessed as we honor the spirits.

- Pour a little bit of alcohol or Florida Water, and offer some tobacco and whatever else you feel sanctifies the grounds.

- Start playing any music you want while the building process takes place. Drums are one good option, as are acoustic guitar, harmonica, or a simple song, possibly one of the spirituals. Silence is also fine, if you prefer.

- Once the Cairn and Cross is finished, step back and clear up any debris or tools.

- If you want to cast sacred space in any fashion you are familiar with, regardless of tradition, this would be the time to do it.

- Gather folks to the Cairn and Cross, preferably so that everyone is facing it from the front. You can still have a circle of sorts, but having everyone looking at the front of the Cairn and Cross is ideal.

- Hand out to each person one of the taper candles.

- Be sure that three candles are set aside next to the Cairn and Cross.

Have a pre-chosen speaker explain the ritual that is about to begin. You will want to mention that this is a monument to honor Harriet "Mama Moses" Tubman and the spirits of the U.G.R.R. and that you will be blessing by sacred flame and song a grave marker for those who have none. Explain that many who traversed the trails to freedom did not make it to their journey's end, sadly succumbing to many fates: sickness, hypothermia, and for some even death upon recapture. Explain that as you all illuminate the Cairn and Cross you will be consecrating your monument and altar to those very spirits. Explain how many of those who were successful, making it across the River Jordan to the Promised Land, were buried under a simple Cairn and Cross like the one before you all. Further explain that many of those crosses did not survive over time, were desecrated, or were even ploughed over now with homes and parking lots on top of them. Explain that what you all do on this night will bring further illumination, elevation, and love to those spirits of the U.G.R.R. across the lands unmarked and forgotten. Finally, share that every person who places the candle they hold at the monument will receive a blessing from the very spirits you are about to exalt, and they should begin to ponder what they will need healing of, removal of, whatever holds them back, and be prepared for a blessing from spirits who, when glorified and honored, can and will bless one with their love in reciprocity.

This is a good time to tell the story of the Lovers and the eternal connection that the Bride and Groom represent. At the end of the story of the Lovers, mention that this is who the Cairn and Cross is for; they are the example. Now that it has been personalized with story and legacy, the marker will be more impactful to those in attendance.

At this point praise Mama Moses with one of her prayers or spirituals contained within this book. Hail her and ask her to witness your devotion and love for her and her Followers.

At this point have everyone rub themselves down with the candle they hold, explaining that the candles are absorbing whatever it is they do not want or need to rid from their body and spirit. Have everyone rub themselves down at the same time, moving down from their heads, through their torso, arms, and legs, including their entire bodies.

Begin to sing or recite the first verse of the "Niagara Spiritual": "Come ride this train, come walk to freedom, come ride this train, with me." Repeat that over and over, and have everyone recite or sing it continually. While everyone sings, begin to light all the candles in the participants' hands. Whether one person lights each one or folks light their own or share from flame to flame is up to you.

While everyone is holding their illuminated candles and still singing or reciting the "Niagara Spiritual," have a chosen person to go and illuminate the cross. Light one of the tapers set aside, melting a few drops onto the top of the vertical crossbeam and placing the candle into the melted wax. Then do the same for either end of the top of the horizontal beams. After doing this, the candle lighter should step back into the group.

Explain to everyone that they should all go up one, two, or three at a time and add their candle in the same fashion; bottom melted a bit and then placed onto one of the rocks at the base of the cross, while still reciting or singing.

Once everyone has put their candle onto the rocks, all lit and shining, everyone can continue to sing or chant while gazing at the illuminated Cairn and Cross. With the cross itself as well as the rocks illuminated by sacred flame, regardless of how ornate your construction and decoration, it's a fairly spectacular sight. The beauty of an illuminated Cairn and Cross leaves an impression indeed, and those moments when all who created it are looking upon it are the time that many will now reflect on and comprehend what has just been built and consecrated. The story of the Lovers will sink in, the tangible presence of Mama Moses and her Followers will be felt, and you will all become part of an ever-growing sacred tradition of exalting the spirits of the U.G.R.R.

Draw the song/chant to its end, and have everyone gaze in silence.

I have always at this moment thanked everyone for their placing of a candle to light the way for the spirits of the U.G.R.R., so that they can see our devotion is in effect. This will bring about many blessings for those in attendance, and it's good to remind folks that whatever they have transferred to the candle they rubbed themselves down with has been alleviated and taken by the spirits who will heal those who illuminate and honor their legacy. This is what the U.G.R.R. spirits bless us with: freedom of that which binds us and holy light from spirits who fought for freedom alongside their white and black allies, friends and fellow warriors, mystics, healers, and diviners. You honor the entire fabric of the sacred quilt that is the U.G.R.R. spirit world by creating a grave marker for those who have none. In those moments of this work you have been clergy, bestowed funerary rites and a celebration of life, revered and invoked a beautiful and kind family of friends from spirit, and you are blessed.

For an ending I often encourage everyone in attendance to join in singing the spiritual "Oh Freedom." The tradition of singing this spiritual on a place that honors the U.G.R.R. or houses its spirits predates the Cairn and Cross itself and shows who we honor on this night: the freedom seekers, long may their lights shine on.

Once "Oh Freedom" has been completed, this is a time to simply talk among yourselves and enjoy or imbibe. It is a good time for folks to go to the Cairn and Cross by themselves to take it in, say their thanks, and share their love. It's also a time for many to take a photo or two! And why not? It's a beautiful sight. If you were the person who facilitated or organized the working, give yourself a moment now that your work is done to soak up what is transpiring about you: fraternity, communion with spirit, and the sacred voodoo you have manifested. It's a joyful service to create the Cairn and Cross, and you yourself have been blessed.

While folks mill about and enjoy one another's company, I keep an eye on the candles, of course. Sometimes we can stay long enough to see them burn out; other times we simply have to eventually extinguish them. There's no harm in doing so, and we do what we have to do. It's those moments when it was illuminated that were sacred.

If you've cast sacred space, it's good to close it and your voodoo down for this work is done.

This is the general outline for a Cairn and Cross ceremony, but there is still plenty of room for your own adaptations and creativity. If you create a Cairn and Cross—and I truly hope you do, as it's the greatest testament we can do for the spirits—then you will have most assuredly already read this book and have a pretty good sense of what's appropriate to add in any way you see fit.

When it comes to the altar arranged beside this work, you can absolutely place offerings of sustenance among the photos or sigil, along with water or alcohol. In the many years of this voodoo, I for the most part do not spray the Cairn and Cross itself, for the amount of heat, light, and love delivered with the intent of those acting in unison is already a very tangible and formidable offering, one that will be felt in more than the spirit world.

Locations to Erect a Cairn and Cross

Now that we know the particulars and the overall impact of creating a Cairn and Cross for a group of people, here are a couple of particular places where they can be erected with a little less fanfare and ceremony, but no less sacred intent. For these situations candles are not a necessity—just the Cairn and Cross itself of any size will do the trick.

ABANDONED CEMETERIES

There are many a location known and unknown sadly in most states and provinces of North America that house the dead travelers of the U.G.R.R. It is our duty as workers in this tradition to continue to heal, in life and for those in the hereafter. So whether the cemetery has marked graves or the grave sites are in an empty field, a parking lot, or a park of some sort, erecting a Cairn and Cross will empower their legacy. Use your discretion, but to place one upon grounds that house the dead if they have no marker, especially in the locations of those that died enslaved or trying to escape, as well as those that made it to freedom, heals a wound and makes a wrong a sacred right.

I, as well as many colleagues, have placed a Cairn and Cross upon such spots, albeit one that will most assuredly at some point be taken down or wrecked. It may not even be legal or encouraged at these places to put up just a small Cairn and Cross, but in my line of work I do what needs to be done at times. The more of us of every color who recognize these places, the more we empower their legacy. There has been more than one location where folks simply continued erecting a Cairn and Cross or placing offerings at an unrecognized spot and this has actually led to an official marker being put up there. This is a true blessing if achieved. While it's not common, of course, it will never happen should we just let those locations continue to be ignored, driven over, and walked on.

Once you understand the mystery contained in the Cairn and Cross, you can erect a simple one just a few feet in height of plain branches tied together quite quickly, especially if you do prior preparations at home to get ready—or when you return home should you just come across a location, which has happened to me many times while traveling. It is our duty as workers in this tradition to continue to heal, in life and for those in the hereafter. If you are a person of color or of African American descent, then coming armed with the voodoo of the Cairn and Cross opens up a new way to revere and honor those of your people who lay forgotten at whatever location. Your simple arrival and introduction are literally familial. For those of any other ethnicity, when arriving at one of these abandoned houses, you will need to approach with a slightly different introductory process. You will want to announce yourself as a "friend," one who is a conductor for the U.G.R.R., for the tracks still run in spirit. You will want to convey your respect for the struggle that once was and for the struggle that continues to this day. Tell them you are creating a marker for them on this spot that has none and you do so in love and respect. If possible a good libation of any sort will also go a long way, for there is surely many a thirst that needs quenching.

Friends and colleagues of color that I am close with have erected a Cairn and Cross at already marked locations for the dead who died enslaved. By erecting a Cairn and Cross on those locations they are celebrating and reminding those spirits that freedom was eventually achieved. It also brings the various spirits of the U.G.R.R. to that very land, where they will embrace their kin in spirit, heal their wounds and broken hearts, and induct them into the spiritual fraternity while bringing life and love to a house of the dead. This is sacred work, and if we do not do it, no one will. This can also be done at locations that house abolitionists, or where their plaques are, or various properties associated with sheltering freedom seekers. It's again a way to remind the spirits that their work was not in vain and we honor their struggle and the struggle that continues in our complex society. In the section for John W. Jones, the Sexton, there is a bit more information on what to do when we come across an abandoned, desecrated, or neglected cemetery.

THE GATEKEEPERS

Abandoned cemeteries present a unique working: honoring the gatekeeper. Every house of the dead is guarded by a denizen spirit, a gatekeeper. This entity carries out a thankless sacred job—unacknowledged except for the attention of sextons, conjurers, and witches who recognize them as we enter any graveyard. In cemeteries where people visit and bring offerings and commune with their dead, the gatekeeper, who sees all from afar, is empowered and fed by their devotion. But even when graves have been abandoned, neglected, or buildings set upon them, the gatekeeper still stands guard. At these abandoned sites, the gatekeeper grows weak, yet stays true.

While working with the sacred practice of building Cairn and Cross monuments, always acknowledge the gatekeeper who is surely standing guard. Even in a shopping mall parking lot, the gatekeeper will hold his vigil. By this act, you bring renewed strength to that denizen; you reinvigorate it. Tell the gatekeeper how good it is that it remains and how much you respect that spirit and its tireless work. By doing so you help empower that very house of the dead as well. Praise the gatekeeper and leave him some change. Whether it be pennies, nickles, or dimes, pay him for his sacred work; in doing so you bring blessings to and receive blessings from the forgotten dead. When I enter any cemetery, whether it be official, neglected, or abandoned, I carry out the same formula: at the threshold of where the graveyard begins, I stop and announce myself as well as knock three times if there is an actual gate present. I say: "Gatekeeper, I honor you and your tireless work. I enter your yard with love and respect for those you guard well and mean no harm to any. Accept a token of my respect." I then offer pennies, a dribble of liquor, sometimes fruit or candy, or a flower—and sometimes all of them. If you cannot do this because you have come across a cemetery unexpectedly and have nothing at hand, then at the very least announce yourself and recognize the gatekeeper before entry. I also always thank him for not only his work but protection as I leave.

A gatekeeper guarded the dead on the very Promised Land in Canaan North, across the River Jordan, where I first encountered the spirits of the U.G.R.R. on that city-owned plot of land behind the BME Church. That gatekeeper guarded the holiest and most historic dead, those who fought and survived on the trails of freedom, with friends and kin of Mama Moses herself resting there. He guarded that plot when no one else even knew there were still brave souls laying beneath. He was the guard of those who entered my home and showed me the way to their spirit world and into the light of Mama Moses. Those spirits were friends of mine.

When their bodies were taken away to God knows where in 2016, when the city finally excavated the grounds for future construction, with their "hired" archaeologists on site (the city and region officially denies any bodies were found, but I was not the only one who watched it happen), I had to bid farewell to their guard and released their gatekeeper, and I did shed a tear in doing so. With the land now empty, the gatekeeper's job had come to a close. I had to release that which was invoked over 150 years ago and had kept the faith for all that time. Wherever those remains now lay, by the grace of God and our work their lights shine on. Reflected down to us from the North Star, their lights shine on. Those spirits are of course still friends of mine, but they will need tending to for a bit, for their place of rest and bodies was desecrated yet again. But they are good, and maybe they will even visit you one night.

Still, guess what? Right across the street is yet another gatekeeper, of another denomination and house of the dead no less holy and sacred. For those are the grounds of the original site of the historic Zion Baptist Church, whose people—albeit just a few—still rest unmarked in the Promised Land under a gravel parking lot and an adjacent backyard or two—that is, shy of the occasional Cairn and Cross that gets erected and re-erected above them, till someone takes it down. What will become of that plot and those who lay beneath? No one knows.

Wherever you are as you do the work, know that because of us, no matter where the forgotten lay, their lights still shine on.

AN INDOOR CAIRN AND CROSS

Although the ceremony shared here describes creating an outdoor Cairn and Cross for a group of people, we can still house one indoors and in our homes. This is of course optional, especially with space being an issue for many, but we can indeed create one of any size to sit upon any shrine or altar for the U.G.R.R. spirits. Creativity and skill with arts and crafts can come into play here. I have one such indoor Cairn and Cross on one of my shrines that is about a foot and a half in height with rocks made from Styrofoam balls glued together and painted and a small wooden cross inserted into this. I have seen ones made with small rocks and a small cross. It really depends on where you want to house it and what you have at hand. No matter the material, if you create a three-dimensional Cairn and Cross, it is an actual marker and serves the same purpose: to honor the spirits of the U.G.R.R. who lay unmarked and to act as a beacon to the spirits who will see you have created a monument for them.

One newer addition to indoor Cairn and Crosses—and something I now do in my home—is to place battery-operated tea lights on the sections of the cross that would hold a candle if it were outdoors. These will not add an actual sacred flame and its heat to the energy of your monument, but many cultures do indeed enlist the beauty of what electric or battery lights have to offer. You can also place small candles around any indoor Cairn and Cross you make, even if you are also utilizing battery-operated candles. I assure you the spirits respond.

One of my fellow Dragon Ritual Drummers has created a three-foot indoor Cairn and Cross, with large Styrofoam balls painted and glued together, and it has served us well when presenting a ceremony at indoor conferences where open candle flames are simply not possible. This particular one is so large and portable it even works with battery-operated tea lights among the faux rocks to emulate a true one illuminated by flame. Sometimes good decoration and ambiance can go a long way.

If you decide to build an indoor Cairn and Cross of any material you have or can work with, the formula is the same. One can certainly do a large Cairn and Cross ceremony as previously described indoors. You would just have to decide how you will create one, what materials you'd like to use, and know that with a bit of creativity and the previous formula, you will be honoring the spirits and everything the Cairn and Cross stands for. It will still be a beneficial voodoo, and the work will still be sacred.

Daguerreotype of John Brown in Springfield, Massachusetts, 1846–47, by Augustus Washington

The Conjuration of "Captain" John Brown

I will raise a storm in this country that shall not be stayed so long as there is slave on its soil.

—LOUIS A. DeCARO, JR., *"FIRE FROM THE MIDST OF YOU:"*
A RELIGIOUS LIFE OF JOHN BROWN

I n the U.G.R.R. spirit world John Brown is the Captain, an officer in the army he would raise to battle against slavery. In his holy army he saw Mama Moses as their General, their beacon and their guide. To some the Captain was a holy martyr, to others a terrorist. Although his hands were bloody, his ardor for ending slavery has marked the ages. He was righteous, devout, and a mystic; he was Captain John Brown.

John Brown's Early Years

John Brown was born on May 9, 1800, in Torrington, Connecticut. In 1805 his family moved from Connecticut to Hudson, Ohio, where John's father, Owen Brown, ran a tannery. The Brown family was Evangelical, and John's parents instilled a strong antislavery foundation in him by aiding many escapees. The U.G.R.R. was already in full effect, and a route came right through Hudson, where the family did their part in a town that did much to support the movement. When John was sixteen, he moved back to New England. Following his religious heart, he began training as a Congregationalist minister; but health and money issues sent him back to Ohio and the family tannery.

In 1820 John Brown married his first wife, Dianthe Lusk, and they moved to Pennsylvania, where they would live for the better part of ten years. John opened his own tannery and raised livestock, and Dianthe bore him seven children. In 1832 Dianthe passed away. A year later John Brown married Mary Ann Day, who eventually bore him thirteen more children.

During this time Brown took much inspiration for his antislavery positions from both Denmark Vesey and his efforts for "the rising" and Nat Turner and his "war." He also admired Toussaint Louverture and his successful tactics in leading the Haitian Revolution. But it was in 1837, upon the murder of abolitionist and Presbyterian minister Elijah P. Lovejoy in Illinois by a proslavery mob, when John Brown would publicly dedicate himself to begin his fight against not only slavery but those who supported it.

> Here, before God, in the presence of these witnesses, from this time, I consecrate my life to the destruction of slavery!
>
> —JOHN BROWN IN STEPHEN B. OATES, *TO PURGE THIS LAND WITH BLOOD*

Brown was also well aware of the insurrection aboard the Spanish ship *La Amistad* off the coast of Cuba in 1839, when Joseph Cinqué and fifty other captured Africans overran the slave ship. They hoped to sail back to the west coast of Africa, only to end up on the shores of Long Island. Their case became a national sensation as pro- and antislavery views were fought out in court. The men were eventually granted their freedom to return to their homeland as at that time it was illegal for slave ships to enter a United States port—even if slavery was of course still legal in America. We can certainly see that a future storm was brewing.

By 1846 John Brown and his family moved to Springfield, Massachusetts, renowned for harboring progressive thinkers, churches, and institutions staunch in their abolitionism. It was in Springfield, as a parishioner of St. John's Congregational Church, founded by a black abolitionist, that John Brown witnessed speeches by both Frederick Douglass and Sojourner Truth. St. John's was no ordinary church and these were no ordinary meetings: this pulpit was one of the most prominent places in America for abolitionist speeches and sermons. John Brown was able to meet face-to-face and discuss into the wee hours of the night plans and points of view with many of the esteemed guests. In particular he would begin a several-year friendship, angst-ridden as it may have been at times, with the greatest American antislavery orator Frederick Douglass.

Their meetings and night-long discussions foreshadowed how future events would play out, for when it came to Brown's position and opinions on the matter of slavery and how to overcome it, a peaceful resolution seemed to be the furthest thing from his mind. As quoted in W. E. B. Du Bois's biography of John Brown, Douglass said in his writings, "While I continued to write and speak against slavery, I became all the same less hopeful for its peaceful abolition. My utterances became more and more tinged by the color of this man's strong impressions."

John Brown and his unique approach helped shape Springfield in his time there into one of the safest and most storied stops for freedom seekers where they could rest while traveling the Underground Railroad. It was also during this time that he conceived of his own militant arm of the Underground Railroad called the Subterranean Pass-Way, a concept for a literal highway along the tops of the Appalachians to funnel armed slaves by the thousands into the North. In Springfield he not only helped solidify already existing safe houses and their ways and means but also formed the League of Gileadites. Embracing his fate to wage a war on slavery, Brown gathered his all-black League of Gileadites to resist the newly passed Fugitive Slave Act, a federal law stating that any runaway was to be captured and returned to the plantation or property he or she had fled by any and all law enforcement, even in the free states, as well as authorizing the prosecution of those who aided in escapes. The League of Gileadites was inspired by those considered the bravest of Israelites who gathered on Mount Gilead to defend their nation from invaders. Due to the actions of the League of Gileadites, not one freedom seeker was recaptured or returned to slavery from within Springfield's city limits.

Brown also drew divine inspiration from Ecclesiastes 4:1, which says, "Again I saw all the oppressions that are done under the sun. Behold the tears of such oppressed and they had no comforter, and on the side of their oppressors there was power; but they had no comforter." It kindled the flame inside his soul to fight slavery at any cost and by any means. It shed divine light upon the evils of oppression by none other than the Lord's words in the Lord's holy book of laws.

John Brown and his family relocated to central New York State to land granted by abolitionist Gerrit Smith for poor black men, and this region and homestead became a breeding ground for the Captain's future plans and the war he would soon start. Having already decided at the very least to organize planned raids to punish and cripple slaveholding regions economically as well as the slavers themselves, Brown was also planting seeds with the free black men of North Elba for his desired course of action: armed insurrection. In North Elba, he and his black allies studied slave revolt tactics, as well as the communities of fugitives known as "maroons," in particular the known ones sheltering in the Great Dismal Swamp of Virginia and North Carolina. Brown also paid attention to the maroon communities of Jamaica. Already having made trips around New York and New England to raise funds and support for an armed conflict against slavery, his plan was to liberate the enslaved via the Subterranean Pass-Way, bring them north, and train them into a fighting force that would eventually attack slaveholding states and regions while freeing and arming even more fighters. This was the Captain's radical militant mission, and while he was not openly condoned or supported, many northern abolitionists were down with the plan. However, before such an organized agenda could be manifest, divine duty and justice were calling from the territory of Kansas.

Bleeding Kansas

In 1855, John Brown got word from his sons living in Kansas that they were soon to be besieged by proslavery forces, mobs of mostly Missourian mercenaries known as Border Ruffians. These proslavery forces meant to attack and spill blood for their cause. It was the desire of many to try to bring Kansas into the Union as a free state, and it was equally desired by proslavery forces that Kansas would do no such thing. Like a tornado sweeping across the plains, Brown sped to Kansas, gathering support of all kinds along the way.

The first Kansas town to be sacked by a proslavery mob was Lawrence. Buildings were destroyed but no lives lost. Still, the era known as "Bleeding Kansas" had begun. Brown was disappointed that the people of Lawrence did not fight back. He preached the biblical eye for an eye and fighting fire with fire, and so he decided to raise the stakes considerably.

Within days Brown and his supporters were calling themselves "The Army of the North" and sought vengeance by attacking the proslavery town of Pottawatomie Creek, in what might be considered a massacre. The Army of the North, predominantly armed with spears and swords, stormed homes of prominent proslavers, dragging them out into the street and hacking them to death. This resulted in a back-and-forth series of battles and guerrilla warfare foreshadowing the American Civil War mere years later. Captain Brown and his ragtag Army of the North at times outfought and outsmarted much larger forces who were always in pursuit. His prowess as a tactician and guerrilla fighter solidified his legend and cult status as the Captain. After many months of skirmishes, two of John Brown's sons were captured, later to be freed, and another son was killed.

Captain Brown left Kansas during a cease-fire of sorts, but Kansas continued to bleed as Brown went east again with three sons in tow and was welcomed as a hero among abolitionists both black and white, albeit now officially with bloodstained hands. For the next two to three years John Brown stumped extensively throughout New England, New York, Pennsylvania, and Ohio, promoting his antislavery narrative, at times traveling under an alias. Through those years he was also heavily focused on a new plan to force the hand of God against the slave states. His fateful raid on Harpers Ferry, Virginia, was taking shape as a well-considered scheme. His planning would bring him to his next fateful trip—to Canada to spend time with Harriet "Mama Moses" Tubman.

The Captain and the General Meet

Historians still debate how and where John Brown crossed into Southern Ontario, then called Upper Canada, but he came to St. Catharines for a purpose: to seek the counsel and forge a bond with the "wanted dead or alive" Mama Moses. The Captain had been aware of her through his abolitionist colleagues, and he was intrigued. He felt they were meant to fight together and that God himself had cast that fate—and he was not the only one. Harriet Tubman had already had visions and premonitions of their coming together. Mama Moses described one of these visions this way:

> I was in a wilderness sort of place, all rocks and bushes, when a big snake raised his head from behind a rock, and while I looked, it changed into the head of an old man with a long white beard on his chin, and he looked at me wishful like, just as if he was going to speak to me. Before he could speak, a crowd of men rushed in and struck him down, while "the old man" looked at me so wishful (Catherine Clinton, *Harriet Tubman: The Road to Freedom*).

She had the same dream several times before their historic meeting.

But as discussed previously, the free slave quarter of St. Catharines, anchored by the BME Church and Zion Baptist house of prayer, was not a place for strangers, especially white ones, to enter unannounced or uninvited—not even the notorious Captain John Brown. He and his entourage spent days in St. Catharines at a saloon awaiting their summons. Then one day an emissary came: it was time to meet Mama Moses. Having lived on the very block where this days-long meeting took place, I am always captivated by what it must have been like: the hardened warrior and self-proclaimed Captain with his fellow soldiers meeting and breaking bread with Mama Moses and her equally formidable warrior circle in their enclave. I assure you the very grounds still hum and shiver. This was thunder meeting lightning, hailstorm meeting tornado, and the plans shared and hatched were the stuff of armed rebellion, uprising, and divine retribution.

Brown's plan to attack and empty the arsenal of Harpers Ferry was what Mama Moses was all about, and she was all in. She promised to enlist as many free black men as possible and was fully intending on being there during the raid. The two warrior circles spent weeks traveling together with some of Canada's most radical abolitionists and supporters, visiting the villages of escaped freedom seekers who had put down roots in Ontario. American abolitionists showed up as well with lots of money and willingness to donate toward their insurrection and came along for the ride, including none other than Mary Ellen Pleasant (more on her later), who also ventured north. They were planning a divine war, and by all accounts excitement and enthusiasm reigned.

This consultation between the Captain and Mama Moses is indeed enshrouded in mystery, but at its end, as the Captain was set to embark south to continue raising an army and the funds to carry out its work, the two mystics exchanged their goodbyes. It was then, here in St. Catharines on the grounds of the BME Church, that the Captain proclaimed that this tiny black woman would be the "General" in their army and war. It was a spiritual proclamation not to be underestimated. The Captain had that much respect for Mama Moses, he was that impressed, and the feeling was mutual. He said he would call to her as General Tubman three times to invoke her presence and blessing when they were no longer together. She loved her title and did so till her final days. The Captain left bidding her Godspeed, and they never saw each other again.

It seems appropriate to jump back to Mama Moses briefly here, for the time the General and the Captain spent together reveals quite a bit. The narrative of Harriet Tubman as a peaceful woman is easily toppled when we see how much she condoned, supported, and wanted to join in the raid on Harpers Ferry. She did not shy away from allying herself with the Captain who had already taken the lives of proslavery supporters. Mama Moses clearly did not flinch at his tactics. And why should this be a surprise? We have two individuals filled with religiosity, two mystics that believed God himself was maneuvering them and their fates. They both believed in the Bible and its teaching to extract justice by an eye for an eye.

This indeed is what we who work with the spirits of the U.G.R.R. must remember: many of them, especially the mystics, lived the words of the Bible in a literal sense. They manifested it with all their might—and why not? In their view certain men who wore the robe and kept the house of Jesus Christ did so allowing the travesty and tyranny of bondage to exist and continue, condoning the normalcy of rape, murder, and enslavement. So in the eternal battle of right and wrong based on the Holy Christian Bible, who is just and who is wicked? Right or wrong depended on one's point of view, and the soul of humanity was at stake. All is fair. Divine justice must be invoked. Slavery must be defeated. The enslaved must have their "comforter." The Captain and the General were in agreement on what must be done at any cost; the divine had instructed the righteous.

Harpers Ferry and the Martyrdom of John Brown

Harpers Ferry, Virginia, housed an armory for the U.S. military of some 100,000 muskets and rifles. John Brown meant to steal them all, distribute them among the locally enslaved, and begin a march south liberating and arming more and fighting those who opposed them. He meant to literally drain Virginia of her slaves. Almost a year in advance of the raid, Brown had had a colleague infiltrate the town of Harpers Ferry to gather intelligence and get a sense of the place. One of the unique things his spy had learned was that the great grandnephew of George Washington was living very close to town and had in his possession two pistols that were given to George Washington by France's Marquis de Lafayette, as well as a sword from Frederick the Great. The pistols and the sword in particular were talismans as far as Brown was concerned—certainly items with unique symbolism in relation to the founding of the United States.

Captain Brown continued to raise funds for the raid, with Mary Ellen Pleasant and his gang of "The Secret Six" of influential and wealthy abolitionists who agreed slavery would not die peacefully, those supporting Brown's mission being the largest donors. Brown assembled through donation some 900 pikes and 200 rifles. His vision for the attack on the armory was of some 4,000 men. As the days ticked down into hours before the attack, he assembled his actual force of twenty-one men. His "army" consisted of sixteen white men and five black men, who would come to be hailed as the Immortal Raiders. No one truly knows why Mama Moses did not arrive at the planned rendezvous or appointed time—nor the fighting force she was to have brought.

As the raid had become a terribly kept secret—to the point of threats by some to expose it—many tried to talk Brown out of executing it, including his friend and confidant Frederick Douglass. Douglass certainly supported the principle, but he also thought it was a suicide mission. He even talked many black men out of joining the attack force, he was so certain it would be futile.

On the morning of October 17, 1859, the raid began. The attack started out well enough for the twenty-one men: they cut telegraph wires, met barely any resistance, and captured the armory, getting word to local slaves that their liberation was coming and to await the signal. They also took hostages including George Washington's great grandnephew, along with his historic pistols and talisman of a sword. But it all went downhill when a baggage master tried to warn an approaching train entering the Harpers Ferry station. He was shot down as the first casualty of the raid; ironically, he was a free black man.

For some reason the train was allowed to continue on, and by the next day the word was out. Local business owners and militia surrounded the armory and pinned down Brown and his force. The armory, which would come to be called "John Brown's Fort," was enveloped by a company of U.S. Marines commanded by none other than Robert E. Lee, then a colonel, within two days. The Marines charged and recovered the armory in little time, killing ten of the Immortal Raiders, including two of Brown's sons.

Taking the Captain alive required a short bout of hand-to-hand combat—in which a divine miracle appeared to manifest. Perhaps it was due to the fact that one of the Marines had mistakenly brought his dress sword and not the one for combat. Or perhaps it was the very buckle attaching George Washington's sword to Brown's body. Whatever the case, when the Marine went in for a death strike, his sword snapped. This exchange slowed and stopped the fighting, and there was silence. John Brown, while injured, was taken alive. Captain Brown did feel that the sword was a talisman and had brought good luck to the raid. Had he been struck down during the raid, many believe he would not have become the martyr he would following his capture, trial, and hanging. So however it is divined, that sword did quite possibly change Brown's fate that day—and the fate of a nation. Found upon his person while taken prisoner were correspondence and money from Mary Ellen Pleasant.

For nearly two months of incarceration, the Captain corresponded with his wife and family. He even refused a well-planned scheme to break him out and steal away north. The Captain would be martyred—many believed it had been his plan all along. During his trial he took full advantage of the platform to challenge slavery and its horrors, causing sensational national headlines. Many from various levels of government asked for him to be spared the gallows.

Upon his conviction he offered these words:

Had I so interfered in behalf of the rich, the powerful, the intelligent, the so-called great, or in behalf of any of their friends, either father, mother, brother, sister, wife, or children, or any of that class, and suffered and sacrificed what I have in this interference, it would have been all right; and every man in this court would have deemed it an act worthy of reward rather than punishment. This court acknowledges, as I suppose, the validity of the law of God. I see a book kissed here which I suppose to be the Bible, or at least the New Testament, that teaches me that all things whatsoever I would that men should do to me, I should do even so to them. It teaches me, further, to "remember them that are in bonds, as bound with them." I endeavoured to act up to that instruction. I say, I am yet too young to understand that God is any respecter of persons. I believe that to have interfered as I have done as I have always freely admitted I have done in behalf of His despised poor, was not wrong, but right. Now, if it is deemed necessary that I should forfeit my life for the furtherance of the ends of justice, and mingle my blood further with the blood of my children and with the blood of millions in this slave country whose rights are disregarded by wicked, cruel, and unjust enactments, I submit; so let it be done!

John Brown was sentenced to be hanged for treason against the state of Virginia.

On December 2, 1859, the hanging was witnessed by the likes of Stonewall Jackson, John Wilkes Booth, and the poet Walt Whitman. Brown refused all ministrations by the clergy at hand, whom he said were stained by their support of slavery or at least their ambivalence toward it. On the way to his gallows he handed a black man a piece of paper on which was written, "I, John Brown, am now quite certain that the crimes of this guilty land will never be purged away but with blood."

His corpse was placed in his coffin with the noose still around his neck and sent north to his wife. John Brown's body rests at his homestead in North Elba, New York, on the grounds of the John Brown Farm, now a New York State Historic Site.

We see a man in John Brown who took the fight against slavery to an extreme level, and while his tactics were called radical, fanatical, and madness by even some of his supporters, he was mourned and celebrated as a martyr by just about the entire abolitionist movement, in the Americas as well as the Caribbean. He invoked righteous justice via the Holy Christian Bible and its laws. We see a man in John Brown who could not stand by and allow injustice to continue any longer, and someone who challenged the very church and state that tried to play both sides of what was truly horrific. We see a man who was a mystic, believing God was guiding him toward a righteous battle for the soul of a nation, while also relying on portents, talismans, and divine intervention. John Brown was a warrior, a holy storm in motion, and like all storms unpredictable and dangerous. But we also see a man with tremendous compassion, who loved his fellow man, woman, and child, and he was gentle to his wives and children. We see a spiritually complex man. For all his religiosity—bordering on zealotry—his admiration for the African-born and their religions as well as the vodou-fueled revolution in Haiti shows quite a bit about his worldview and a respect for the personal nature of one's religion and the values it invokes from within. He was a Captain, one who commanded a company of soldiers, and in his army his soldiers followed him even unto their death. His battle against slavery cost him and three of his sons their lives, and his martyrdom lit the literal fuse that would explode into the American Civil War. If there is a spirit of the U.G.R.R. whose martyrdom elevates him to a level comparable to "folk saint," it is Captain John Brown. He sacrificed himself when there was a viable option to escape and live to fight another day. Harriet Tubman said of the Captain, "He done more in dying, than 100 men would in living (Clifford, *Bound for the Promised Land*)."

> So there was hail, and fire flashing continually in the midst of the hail,
> very severe, such as had not been in all the land of Egypt
> since it became a nation.
>
> —Exodus 9:24

The Elevation of Captain John Brown

The Captain was a martyr—and a holy one at that. He was mourned by many and even elevated to the level of a Christlike figure by the transcendentalists of the time. Soon after his death he was immortalized in the ballad "John Brown's Body," his legacy sung by black Union soldiers as they went marching into battle. His former homestead in North Elba, New York (Lake Placid), is a historical site that is visited by many. People make pilgrimage to his grave and surrounding lands to ponder his sacrifice and place in history. The location of hanging at the Gibson-Todd House in Charles Town, West Virginia, is also a historical site, and another introspective pilgrimage point. In Harpers Ferry, a plaque states, "Here

John Brown aimed at human slavery a blow that woke a guilty Nation. With him fought seven slaves and sons of slaves. Over his crucified corpse marched 200,000 black soldiers and 4,000,000 freedmen singing 'John Brown's body lies a-mouldering in the grave, but his soul goes marching on.'" Statues of him stand at the John Brown Memorial at Quindaro Townsite, Kansas City, Kansas, and at the John Brown Farm. This is all a tangible "folk" canonization. Shorty after his death by hanging, John Brown was immortalized by the leaders of Haiti, when they named a street in their capital of Port-au-Prince after him in solidarity with his aims. It still stands, and his soul goes marching on.

Every time one discusses the legacy of General Tubman in certain veins, one is sure to find the Captain not far behind. They are still profoundly connected in the afterlife, along with their colleagues, fellow soldiers of freedom, and their family descendants to this day. Several black churches and fraternities recognize the anniversary of John Brown's martyrdom, December 2, as a significant day, wrapped and cloaked in various mysteries. He is said to haunt many of the sites where he lived and also the spot where he died, from his homestead in New York to right here in St. Catharines—to which I can testify.

Working with Captain John Brown

Captain John Brown can be called on for many reasons, not only as a true comforter and protector, but as an equalizer as well as a champion. We call to John Brown when we need to invoke a holy storm for our just cause, to lay siege to those who mean us harm, for the Captain still engages in guerrilla tactics from spirit. And as with Mama Moses, the Captain does not always arrive alone. He comes at times with his formidable fellow warriors who fought and died for his holy war: his band of Immortal Raiders, the Army of the North, or members of his all-black League of Gileadites. When we work with the Captain's spirit, we are invoking at times a true army of Immortal Raiders on our behalf—and they do answer.

While we can honor the Captain at any time we see fit, there is a unique fluidity that presents itself while storms are arriving wherever we live. The storm is a doorway to his warrior nature, his strength, and his ability to scorch the earth upon thine enemies—or at the very least give you the support and inspiration to conjure such into manifestation. He can be a great counsel when we are faced with inevitable conflict, for the Captain was a tactician and studied warfare. Whether it was conventional, guerrilla, or psychological, he was skilled in them all, so the Captain provides incredible advice when summoned while we are faced with hostility.

His warrior nature aside, you should be cautious in invoking him and his accompanying Immortal Raiders to aid in a conflict. We should only do so when our cause is surely just. Even in view of his fiery nature, the Captain and his warriors are not to be utilized for curses or to cause harm to those we simply have a dislike toward. Trying to do so will simply generate a sense of disappointment from his tangible spirit. You would be better off invoking him for his counsel in the midst of adversity—from which he can and will deliver you.

As we have seen, the Captain was more than just a righteous fighter; he was devout. John Brown was a holy man of sorts; he just doled out the Holy Spirit in his own unique way, delivering baptisms by fire and blood, and so we cannot forget his impressive knowledge of the Bible and its laws. He was a man who studied scripture, and for those immersed in Christian conjure, he can bestow upon you knowledge of certain scriptures, psalms, and prayers in ways you may not have previously seen or understood. This is the gentle and compassionate side of the Captain's spirit, one that accompanies us while reading scripture, and his spirit can reveal mysteries contained within the Bible we need to see at times, in a form similar to bibliomancy, which we will look at soon.

His connection in life to many of the Pillars of Freedom carries on tangibly in the hereafter—with Mama Moses, Frederick Douglass, and Mary Ellen Pleasant, to name a few. One other unique affiliation of the Captain's spirit that has not come up in our historical rundown is his adoration of children. A few of my colleagues who have worked with and invoked his spirit have attested to him manifesting to their very children in a harmonious way. This is something I have witnessed in regard to a spiritual brother and Brown's connection to his son. Let's face it, as we have come to learn, the man was prolific in his procreation, siring twenty offspring. He was a lover of all children of all colors and still is to this day. Incidentally, the statue of him at the John Brown Farm in New York State depicts him guiding a freed slave child. There are many complexities to the Captain's spirit, and I encourage you to seek his presence for times not just associated with conflict, but rest assured that when it comes to protecting our homes and spirit and our ability to wield that around us through his tools and conjurations, he is a most effective and beneficial spirit.

Accoutrements and Tools for Captain John Brown

As has been suggested previously, John Brown's image can be placed upon any U.G.R.R. altar, as well as beside any altar or shrine for any of its spirits. One can certainly create an altar or shrine specifically for the Captain, although I can understand it is for many unrealistic to create individual ones for all of the pillars or figures associated with the U.G.R.R. spirit world. But if you do want to create a place of prominence for his spirit, there are ways to accomplish this with his tools of power.

MINIMUM ACCOUTREMENTS

- John Brown's image. There are many photographs of him out there. His portrait in this book is my favorite, for it depicts him in

Springfield mid-vow, holding the standard for the Subterranean Pass-Way.

- A candle to illuminate his space when worked as well as to help sustain his spirit.

- A glass of fresh water. Any space that will be used to call forth the spirits should contain a glass of fresh water for its life force as well as possibly flowers for the same purpose.

TOOLS OF POWER

- A Bible. The Captain was a devout man and a studier of scripture. Note that this can be the Bible you use for all of your U.G.R.R. conjures.

- A Christian cross

- A sword. The weapon of choice for this holy warrior; it is one with significance in the scriptures. He believed such a weapon could possess talismanic properties.

- A knife or dagger. This pragmatic weapon and tool was one he was fond of, and he carried several throughout his life.

- A machete. This is the tool of revolt and uprisings, especially the ones John Brown was inspired by. It would be great to have your working machete as his tool.

- Replica or decorative pistols and guns. For obvious reasons, the Captain was skilled with a gun and took blood and life from the wicked with it. (Optionally, this can be a blessed legal gun, especially an antique if one is so inclined.)

- An axe. This was another tool he used, for both pragmatic purposes as well as weaponry.

- A decorative, replica spear. The Captain was skilled in a form of spear/pike combat and taught it to many who entertained his plans for insurrection and the Subterranean Pass-Way. He amassed nearly 1,000 pikes in preparation for his Harpers Ferry raid.

- A replica, decorative or toy, or image of a horse. If you build a shrine for the Captain, a horse should be there. He was a skilled horseman, and he rode across entire sections of North America on many steeds. He had a deep love for horses, and in fact arrives upon a spectral steed at times, as do some of the Immortal Raiders and Army of the North. This connection could also be honored with various tools or equipment associated with horses—especially a horseshoe.

- Optional: For those that go hard in conjure and recognize a spirit's animal companion, you can also make offerings to the steeds of the Captain and warriors, e.g., carrots, sugar cubes, apples. These will be accepted. This could be done if you have become comfortable enough to summon the Captain to the point of recognizing his steeds or when you have had to invoke his divine storm and warrior magic and want to empower even the beasts on which the spirits ride. Personally, I am one of those who feeds spectral beasts when possible.

When it comes to his tools, and in particular his weaponry, these can be his shrine literally on their own. Place the tools like a sword, blade, axe, or spear somewhere of prominence and focus in your home or at your doorways and entrances as protection. You can always keep his portrait among others on an altar along with a Bible and cross, but his weapons can—and I recommend they should—be tools for protection of your home. You already know how to bless and empower a working machete, and that could indeed be your tool dedicated to the Captain when you need to wield a blade for protection on a magical level. But it doesn't hurt to dedicate a different one for working with the Captain if you are so inclined.

Offerings

As with Mama Moses and her Followers, we can empower our connection to the Captain's spirit and sustain its longevity with some offerings. For the Captain these are minimal. Shy of the previously mentioned fresh water and flowers, a good offering or two could be the following:

- Wine. While the Captain was a professed teetotaler later in life, he was not only fond of wine, but championed its use as "pure," unlike the liquors and spirits of his time that were filled with dangerous additives. And of course wine has religious and biblical significance. This is not to say he was a hard-core drinker of it, even though two of his sons for many years ran a vineyard, but he was known to enjoy a glass now and then. He will not be offended by an offering that is the symbolic blood of Christ.

- Tea. A hot black tea, or even a mild herbal, is a great offering to add to any space where you will enlist his presence for a type of work that would require the extra sustenance.

If you cannot decide which would please him more, leave a small glass of wine as well as a cup of tea and let the Captain decide from which to take energy. Between the wine, tea, and water you will have provided enough to enhance the connection. Another thing to remember is that just like some of Mama Moses' Followers partake of alcohol although she did not herself, the Captain's warriors and other soldiers in spirit would be more than happy to accept an offering of alcohol.

Prayers, Petitions, and Workings

The spirit of John Brown may be invoked by a number of prayers. Petition him when you have a just case against those working against you, and he will be a powerful ally. He will also come to your aid in supplying knowledge on biblical matters and incantations.

PRAYERS TO CAPTAIN JOHN BROWN

When beginning any work with Captain John Brown, it is recommended to read aloud the prayer he recited every morning along with his wife, children, and whomever else was willing and in his presence when he rose before dawn. This prayer is a wonderful offering to him all on its own to appease and please his spirit either upon his arrival or as an invocation to do so.

Remember them that are in bonds as bound with them.

Whoso stoppeth his ear at the cry of the poor,
he also shall cry himself, but shall not be heard.

He that hath a bountiful eye shall be blessed;
for he giveth his bread to the poor.

A good name is rather to be chosen than great riches,
and loving favour rather than silver and gold.

Whoso mocketh the poor reproaches his Maker,
and he that is glad at calamities shall not be unpunished.

He that hath pity upon the poor lendeth unto the Lord,
and that which he hath will he pay him again.

This prayer, taken from scripture as his daily mantra, demonstrates his affirmations focusing on sympathy for the poor and oppressed. This daily recitation still echoes in the spirit world, and when you recite it aloud, he will hear you.

A conjuration for the Captain which is also effective in calling him is his favorite hymn from when he walked the earth. "Blow Ye the Trumpet, Blow" will act as a great invocation as well as honor what brings his spirit joy.

Blow ye the trumpet, blow
The gladly solemn sound; Let all the nations know, To earth's remotest bound,
The year of Jubilee is come; Return, ye ransomed sinners, home.
Extol the Lamb of God, The all-atoning Lamb;
Redemption through his blood Throughout the world proclaim.
The year of Jubilee is come; Return, ye ransomed sinners, home.
The Gospel trumpet hear, The news of heav'nly grace;
And saved from earth appear Before your Savior's face.
The year of Jubilee is come; Return, ye ransomed sinners, home.

The following is a wonderful prayer original to John Brown. First utilized for white children that were in his presence either during sermons or speeches, it was an oath of sorts, and assuredly a blessing he bestowed upon those whose head he would touch while intoning it.

In the name of God, who is your father,
and the father of the African,
In the name of the Son, who is your Savior
and the Savior and master of the African,
In the names of the Holy Spirit, which gives you strength,
and which gives strength and comfort to the African,
I bless thee.
Amen.

A wonderful way to connect with and invoke the spirit of the Captain is to sing or recite the words to either one or both of the ballads that immortalize him and his martyrdom. I have chosen to share a version for this book that I have found to be the most effective when conjuring him.

When you feel you need his presence, this is simple and effective. By this act alone you can connect to his spirit, and when his presence is felt, you should communicate to him the purpose and agenda you have prepared ahead of time. The ballad "John Brown's Body" is powerful and sacred testimony and encapsulates many of his attributes from his holiness to his valor. Simply lighting and holding a candle while reciting "John Brown's Body" is a conjuration, as it was when sung by the black Union soldiers as they marched into battle.

Old John Brown's body lies moldering in the grave,
While weep the sons of bondage whom he ventured all to save;
But tho he lost his life while struggling for the slave,
His soul is marching on.

John Brown was a hero, undaunted, true and brave,
And Kansas knows his valor when he fought her rights to save;
Now, tho the grass grows green above his grave,
His soul is marching on.

He captured Harper's Ferry, with his nineteen men so few,
And frightened "Old Virginny" till she trembled thru and thru;
They hung him for a traitor, themselves the traitor crew,
But his soul is marching on.

John Brown was John the Baptist of the Christ we are to see,
Christ who of the bondmen shall the Liberator be,
And soon thruout the Sunny South the slaves shall all be free,
For his soul is marching on.

The conflict that he heralded he looks from heaven to view,
On the army of the Union with its flag red, white and blue.

And heaven shall ring with anthems o'er the deed they mean to do,
For his soul is marching on.

Ye soldiers of Freedom, then strike, while strike ye may,
The death blow of oppression in a better time and way,
For the dawn of old John Brown has brightened into day,
And his soul is marching on.

When finishing off any working or conjuration for the Captain, an effective bid is this:

I thank you, Captain John Brown,
your soul goes marching on, Godspeed!

THE SWORD OF JUSTICE AND THE ARMOR OF GOD

I will say again for those not of the Christian faith: remember that John Brown was a devout man as were many of the spirits of the U.G.R.R. Also keep in mind that many who were held in bondage used the Bible as a source of incantations. It was to many the only grimoire that was available, and so the words are power for the purposes of conjuration. While this will not be an issue for Christian conjurers or hoodoo practitioners, I would recommend to others that you try the biblical incantations, especially for the first few times in connecting with the Captain. In time you can of course fashion your own invocations, but for starters give the biblical ones a go to establish the connection and appease his spirit. Try it, you might like it! Also remember that Christians of many denominations will find these conjures blasphemous witchcraft and the work of the Devil, so it all depends on where you sit. From where I sit, it's the spirits that need appeasing, and there is no end we should not go to to ensure as much as we taketh we also giveth.

THE ARMOR OF GOD

Safeguard your home with the Armor of God and the protection of Captain John Brown in a manner that has survived as U.G.R.R. conjure in my region.

TOOLS AND MATERIALS

- Two kitchen knives. Whatever kitchen knives you choose—from meat to fish to butter—is up to you. They can be ones you have used for many years or simply do not use—we all have those knives. Or you can purchase new or used ones for this task. The size of the knives matters not; they will soon become blessed and act as the armor of god. If you can use some nice sharp ones that are a bit on the ferocious side, though, that would be ideal.

- A Bible

- A cross

- Jerusalem oil (see p. 72).

- Red ribbon or string, about two feet in length. These will represent the blood of Christ or just sacred blood if that's too Holy Roller for you.

- A candle. Any color or kind is fine.

- A shot of liquor. Rum is best.

EMPOWERING THE ARMOR OF GOD

- Begin by lighting your candle and recite:

> *I light this candle to honor Captain John Brown*
> *and guide him to me in my time of need.*

- Place the candle beside your Bible and cross.

- Recite his morning prayer (see p. 156), and finish off with:

  The stars above in Heaven are looking kindly down on the grave of old John Brown. Hail and welcome, Captain!

- Pick up your two knives, hold one in each hand, and focus on the protection you wish to conjure about your home.

- Recite:

  In truthful speech and in the power of God; with the weapons of righteousness in the right hand and in the left. —2 Corinthians 6:7

- Recite:

  Put on the full armor of God, so that you can take your stand against the devil's schemes. —Ephesians 6:11

- At this time spray your knives with the liquor. One can also rub the blades with the rum as well. You are feeding the very steel that will fight for you and protect your home.

- Now tie the two blades together with the red ribbon/string in an "X" fashioned like an X-shaped St. Andrew's Cross. It will take a lot of string or ribbon to get this done; intertwining between the blades, both vertically and horizontally as in lashing, so be as patient as you can while also being careful not to cut yourself, and stay focused on the reason you are creating the Armor of God. (If you happen to draw blood, it's not a bad omen; just consider it extra empowerment.)

- When you are done tying the knives together, anoint them with Jerusalem oil, rubbing some on both sides of the blades in a cross motion, saying the Jerusalem oil prayer: "As the mountains surround Jerusalem, so the Lord surrounds his people, from this time forth and forevermore" (Psalm 125:2).

- When you are done, kiss the center of the blades where they have been tied together, and say: "I kiss thee, my Armor of God."

- Hold the tied knives high and recite: "Harness the horses, And mount the steeds, And take your stand with helmets on! Polish the spears, Put on the scale-armor!" (Jeremiah 46:4).

- Take your Armor of God and place it above your front or back door, attaching it in any way you can, whether that is mounted on the wall above the door or sitting on the ledge above it. Just be sure it forms an "X." If this is not possible for some reason, then a windowsill is also an acceptable place to set the Armor of God. The points of the knives should be facing down, pinning your enemies' efforts as they try to enter your dwelling, as well as a traditional way swords are placed in victory. The "X" shape is crossing off and sealing your home of negativity and bad juju being thrown toward you.

- Finish off by standing before your placed Armor of God and reciting: "I ask you, Captain John Brown, and your immortal warriors to always encircle my home with protection from those wicked ones who mean me harm. Bless my Armor of God and draw thine swords as you see fit. I thank you, Captain John Brown. Let your soul go marching on, Godspeed!"

Of course, you can add any other form of protection to your doorways, as I'm sure many do and will, but the Armor of God is a great conjure to bring forth the protection of the Captain of the U.G.R.R. spirit world as well as his immortal warriors. You can also place the Armor of God beside or near the quilt code sigil of the Drunkards Path (see p. 227), as it is also a great ward to be placed above doorways. It's best to reup the working at least a couple of times a year, or as you see fit based on your own regimen of home protection. All my doorways have the Armor of God above them.

THE SWORD OF JUSTICE

When you feel you need to invoke some hard justice for yourself or a loved one—although, again, you must scrutinize your conscience before taking this step—then this is a petition for the Captain to help you wield the Sword of Justice. This is for when you know someone is working against you and it needs to not only be stopped but defeated.

MATERIALS AND TOOLS

- A sword, large knife, or blade. Even a kitchen knife will do, and in fact the kitchen knife was a traditional tool for this work. That being said, your machete would also be great for this working, so be sure to read the section on the machete to familiarize yourself with that tool (see p. 65).

- A Bible

- A cross

- A candle. Any kind or color will do.

- Images/pictures/photos of or the names written out of the people you know are throwing bad magic your way.

- Jerusalem oil (see p. 72).

- A shot of liquor. Rum is best.

INVOKING THE SWORD OF JUSTICE

- Light your candle and recite: "I light this candle to honor Captain John Brown, and guide him to me in my time of need."

- Place the candle beside your Bible and cross.

- Recite any of the Captain's prayers of power or his ballad, and finish off with:

*The stars above in Heaven are looking kindly down on the grave of
old John Brown. Hail and welcome, Captain!*

- Speak aloud of the people and magic you wish to protect your home
  from, and be specific. You are speaking aloud as affirmation and
  intent, for the Captain and whoever is accompanying him to hear,
  as well as to the realm of spirit that surrounds you.

- Hold your chosen blade in front of you and spray it with the liquor.

- Recite:

  *A sword, sharpened and polished—Sharpened to make a slaughter,
  Polished to flash like lightning! —Ezekiel 21:9*

- Recite:

  *If I sharpen My flashing sword, And My hand takes hold on justice,
  I will render vengeance on My adversaries, And I will repay those
  who hate Me. —Deuteronomy 32:41*

- Recite:

  *You fear the sword, and the sword is what I will bring against you.
  —Ezekiel 11:8*

- Finish off the verses by reciting:

  So sayeth me!

- Recite:

  *Captain John Brown, I ask you and your warriors to fight with me.
  Vanquish the enemies whose names I have uttered and their wicked ways;
  enshroud me in God's armor and bless my weaponry.*

- Take the picture or the written names of those you know are working
  against you, pick it up, and stab it, cut it, shred it in any way you see
  fit with your blade. Lay siege upon their efforts. As you slice and cut

them away with your Sword of Justice before the Captain, you are in essence defeating your enemies. Put a little emotion into it, as you should if you have gone to the lengths to do this conjure.

- When done piercing and destroying the image/names of those who are throwing bad magic your way, gather up the fragments and place them together. These should be scattered to the winds outdoors wherever you live, although this does not have to be done right away.

- Take your blade and again feed it with liquor.

- Hold it high and recite:

> *But thanks be to God! He gives us the victory*
> *through our Lord Jesus Christ. —1 Corinthians 15:57*

- Anoint your blade in Jerusalem oil as you recite its prayer:

> *As the mountains surround Jerusalem, so the Lord surrounds his people,*
> *from this time forth and forevermore. —Psalm 125:2*

- Place the blade either by your front or back door, leaning it against the wall, point down. It should stay there till you know the work sent your way has been defeated.

- Recite:

> *I ask you, Captain John Brown, and your warriors to seek out, finish off,*
> *and cut down my enemies we have engaged this night. I honor you and*
> *thank you for your efforts, Captain John Brown.*
> *Your soul goes marching on. Godspeed!*

- Take your fragments of photos/names, which are hopefully pretty messed up from the piercing, cutting, shredding, etc., and throw them outside. Let the fragments be scattered in the wind, blown away, severed, and without burial. Recite: "let ye corpses and souls be ever in the fires of purgatory, so sayeth I!"

- Come inside, give yourself a good cleanse, and leave whatever workspace you created for the Captain illuminated for a while.

- Another form of this work can be done by again having a photo/name written of those you know mean you harm along with your blade of choice, with a sharp point. And if you have access to grass or ground near your home, you can do the following.

- Invoke the captain.

- Bless and praise your sword with one of the incantations.

- Speak of the wickedness that afflicts you and from whom it originates.

- Stab and pierce the photo/name with your blade into the ground, and mess it up good.

- Pick up what remnants you can, and scatter them to the air, saying,

  Let ye corpses and souls be ever in the fires of purgatory, so sayeth I!

- Thank the Captain and God for your impending victory.

Another less stabby and anger-filled way to use—if that's not your style—is available if you have access to a safe spot outdoors, whether in your yard or a place where you can stay at with your sword/machete for about an hour or so. You can pin down the photo or name to the ground with the machete blade and leave it overnight, if possible, or for just an hour or so. Once the photo or written name is pierced into the ground, with your machete upright and stuck into the ground, light a candle and place the candle on the handle as was described in the section for working with your machete (see p. 65). This will empower your blade as it pins down, pierces, and afflicts your enemy. Once the candle has melted down or your work is done, tear the photo or written name or shred it with your machete and scatter the bits to the winds, saying, "Let ye corpses and souls be ever in the fires of purgatory, so sayeth I!"

And finally, another version you can do is follow the same formula, but instead of your machete you can use a railway spike. Feed the spike with liquor as you would the sword and take it outside anywhere, but preferably in a discreet or bushy location, pin down the image or name into the ground, and leave it there, potentially permanently.

SCRIPTURES BY THE CAPTAIN'S STORM

A unique—and dare I say fun—way to interact with not only the Captain, but also with the Bible you have chosen to work with is to commune with them when strong or stormy winds arrive in your region. When a good wind or stormy weather arrives in your area, make a connection to the Captain as best you can or see fit.

- Take your Bible outside into the winds.

- Hold up your Bible and recite:

    Hail, Captain John Brown, he who travels from storm to storm.
    Your soul goes marching on!

- Recite: "Good Captain, man of scriptures, reveal to me that which I should know at this time."

- Place the Bible down on a surface, open it up wherever you feel like, and let the wind do its thing.

- The pages will surely blow about, back and forth, and at some point will stop and stay open.

- Pick the Bible up and read the first lines that jump out at you or whatever part of the page you have chosen to focus on. You can determine ahead of time, if you like, what part of the page you will start from or just go where your eyes are drawn.

- Read aloud what you have been drawn to and focused on, reciting it to the winds that have revealed a mystery to you.

- Mark the page and section, and thank the Captain:

    Thank you, Captain Brown, I will study the words revealed to me. May your soul go marching on. Godspeed!

- Return indoors and revisit the section the Captain and his wind have revealed. Reread and ponder the text.

You can also conjure and invoke the Captain, if you are so inclined, for simple company while reading scripture. If you are not too fond of Bible work but are going to give it a try for sorcery's sake, then for those times you do decide to go in where you prefer not to go, invoke the Captain and ask him to help you find some joy or knowledge as you do so. This is a magic he will be happy to bestow upon you.

The Celestial Gate

A celestial gate, a doorway to the heavens, reveals itself for several days at two different phases of each moon cycle. The moon cycle was of paramount importance to the freedom seekers, as were the starry mysteries of the heavens above. This working is one that has a legacy as a unique and powerful time to pray for miracles, blessings, and life-altering roads of possibility.

As it is waxing, and between the waxing crescent and waxing gibbous phase, the moon will be visible in the sky in the late afternoon as the sun is positioned to set on the opposite side of the sky. For those planning their break for freedom, this was a time to pray for the safe passage that would take upward of a year for some. This is a work I have shared with many over the years, and I do it as often as I can to not only connect myself to the celestial mysteries and moon cycle—which can only make you a stronger conjurer—but to form a tie with Mama Moses and her Followers in a way they also utilized at the gate of infinite prayers.

Work for the Waxing Moon:
Waxing Crescent and Gibbous Phase

- When the moon is in the sky, positioned opposite the sun, spread your legs to shoulder width and focus on your body and spirit firmly grounded here on our earth.

- Take your hand—left or right, depending on your location—and raise it to the sky, palm facing out, to cover the moon.

- Take your other hand and raise it to the sky, palm out, to cover the sun.

- With both your hands now outstretched, close your eyes.

- With your eyes closed and hands raised covering the moon and sun, focus on your feet upon the earth.

- Draw down the moon and sun into your mind, body, and soul, as well as drawing up the earth beneath you.

- Breathe deeply and slowly and focus on the celestial gate you stand between. You are at this moment a crossroads, a gateway between our sacred earth and the moon and sun.

- Envision what it is that you want to manifest.

- Speak aloud, even if only in a whisper, that which you desire or need. Be specific and detailed and know as you offer you words they will go from your lips to God's ears.

- When you feel you have offered your prayer, open your eyes, lower you arms, and breathe slowly and deeply once again. Ground yourself in the earth and make any finishing statement you are comfortable with, be it a "so mote it be," "amen," or "as I speak it, so it shall be."

This is a truly empowering conjure. As moon cycles go, waxing is a time to pray for things coming, things you are building toward and wanting to manifest. The most optimal time to do this is when the moon and sun are equally positioned on opposite sides of the sky, but it is still effective when one is tipped to one side further than the other. As long as you can reach out both hands to cover their view and draw them down, you will still experience a very tangible working.

Work for the Waning Moon: Last Quarter to Waning Crescent

As the moon is waning, from the last quarter to waning crescent phase, which is roughly about eight to nine days from when the moon and sun were last visible in the sky together, is the next time you will be able to do this conjure during the same moon cycle. Only now, instead of the late afternoon to early evening, your window will be in the early to late morning hours, and the moon will now be where the sun was about nine days previously. The sun now as it rises will be positioned where the moon was back at the waxing gibbous phase.

This was a marked event routine for freedom seekers while they were en route toward Canaan and the Promised Land. Since trekking north most often happened at night and under the cover of darkness, this would be a sign to freedom seekers that it was safe to get some necessary sleep. This is the part of the moon cycle immortalized in the conjure symbol of the Cairn and Cross. As moon cycles go, this is a time to work on removing obstacles, dark magic, the mysteries of the Crone, and leaving behind that which does not serve us well. Use the same formula as for the waxing moon, covering the moon and sun with your hands and drawing them both into you as well as the earth below you. The difference in the time of day will undoubtedly be noticeable, subtle as it is, but if you incorporate this into your magical routines, it will only enhance your magic, conjurations, and spellwork while attuning you to the moon's cycles. At the very least, this is a marked moment for you to use a celestial gateway, one between the sun, moon, earth, and you as the gatekeeper, and it's a great time to announce to that gate that which we seek and desire.

As I observe and work this just about every moon, it has taught me, while meandering through time and magic with the spirits, just how long the freedom journeys were. You can feel the expanse between moon cycles as truly as if you were on a constant walk—aware of pursuit with no full rest till Canaan is reached.

Mary Ellen Pleasant

The Conjuration of "Mistress" Mary Ellen Pleasant

I n the spirit world of the U.G.R.R. Mary Ellen Pleasant is the true "Mistress": a woman of authority and control. She wore many other monikers in her time: "Voodoo Queen," "Mother of Civil Rights," and "Black City Hall." She was all of those as well as one of Captain John Brown's biggest supporters personally and financially. She drew particular inspiration from a contemporary she shared time with: Marie Laveau, the Voodoo Queen of New Orleans. A celebrated philanthropist who did things her way and by her rules, she was Mistress Mary Ellen Pleasant.

Mary Ellen Pleasant's Early Years

Mary Ellen Pleasant, a woman of mystery from the very beginning, was born on August 19, somewhere between 1812 and 1814, most likely in Georgia. Her mother was a black Creole woman from Louisiana born and raised, and her father was probably one of the white sons of the then governor of Virginia. Her mother, who was enslaved, was also a Louisiana voodoo practitioner of some renown, as was her mother before her, and voodoo would come to be a defining part of the Mistress's life. Mary Ellen Pleasant was herself born a slave, but her freedom was purchased and she was sent to Nantucket, Massachusetts, as a preteen bonded servant to work for a Quaker woman known as Grandma Hussey. Mary Ellen would work off her indentured servitude as a young woman and actually join the Hussey family, who were renowned abolitionists. Within this household, the Mistress was able to meet some of the most celebrated abolitionists of the time, which had a strong and lifelong effect upon her. The Mistress was able to pass as white, and the Hussey family helped her with that useful trait, which would gain her the favor and privileges available at the time, as well as offer a powerful tool for future U.G.R.R. activities.

While the year is not quite known, she would marry a man named James Smith, who was also a man of color who could pass as white and often did. Smith was a wealthy flour plantation owner who had freed his slaves and an active member of the U.G.R.R. He and Mary Ellen would become celebrated, yet secret "slave stealers," as they were called, funneling freedom seekers to the North via secret routes and funded means right up into St. Catharines. Their wealth and ability to pass had them in the inner circles of the heavy hitters that helped the freedom train run and maintained its tracks. James Smith would pass away after about four years of marriage, leaving Mary Ellen a large fortune along with instructions to maintain it for the purpose of supporting the U.G.R.R.

Somewhere around 1848, Mary Ellen married a second time, albeit in secret to a man named John James Pleasants. They both continued her U.G.R.R. work and slave stealing. They stayed busy enough that they began to catch the attention of slavers and their supporters, which forced them to relocate and hide their tracks. So the two moved to New Orleans and the region of her mother's birth.

It is understood that John James was a relative to Marie Laveau's husband, and that formed Mary Ellen's connection to Marie Laveau. While how they spent their time and what they shared during this period is still debated, voodoo as well as clandestine work to help the enslaved were the components of their sisterhood, if not more accurately a mentorship for Mary Ellen. This is a wondrous and often overlooked aspect of Marie Laveau's legacy—her support in helping slaves in the Crescent City flee for freedom in the North, as well as hatching out with Mary Ellen another viable track to freedom, but this time in the West. This was assuredly a time when Mary Ellen Pleasant continued to hone her skills in voodoo, along with learning how to enlist spies and leverage favors, the coded communication of the South, and philanthropy. And she continued to do so while her husband was off in California to check on its viability as a U.G.R.R. terminus.

After about a year of what some would say was Mary Ellen Pleasant reinventing herself in the fashion of the Voodoo Queen of New Orleans, she too embarked for San Francisco to join her husband circa 1852.

In San Francisco, Pleasant immediately put to use the skills learned under Marie Laveau. She passed as white among whites, but did not conceal her race to fellow blacks. She began to work at exclusive men's clubs that catered to the city's highest echelons, providing entertainment and favors that rich white men were seeking as well as serving them and being in the midst of their gossip. She listened and gained valuable intelligence on how the city worked, who ran it, and how to benefit financially while in earshot of the powerful. She had been an apt pupil of Marie Laveau indeed.

The Mistress also made use of her seemingly invisible blackness to find work and places to live for fugitives at the western terminus of the U.G.R.R. Her new terminus brought an immense number of freedom seekers to California from Louisiana and Texas, hidden among the chaos and immigration of the gold rush. While California was not a slave state, it was not exactly a level playing field for free blacks either; but it was at least a place far from bounty hunters, most of whom were too focused on the tracks leading north from the central and eastern United States. The Mistress's own tracks to freedom and the western gateway terminus were the best-kept secret for many years. Abolitionists and secret circles on the other side of the continent were impressed, as was the holy storm in motion, Captain John Brown.

The Mistress and the Captain

Mary Ellen Pleasant left San Francisco for about two years, between 1857 and 1859, to accept a summons and invitation to join Captain John Brown. She had begun to make immense amounts of money through her spying, leveraging of favors, and the connections she gained in San Francisco, and she wanted to put some of it to good use. She not only donated large sums of money to Captain Brown, but traveled with his unique and colorful entourage under the banner of the Subterranean Pass-Way. She even ventured into Canada, purchasing property to donate to the large freed slave population—whose original escapee inhabitants hailed from Louisiana—in Chatham, Ontario, where she then joined the secret tour of Mama Moses, Captain Brown, and a host of Canadian abolitionists that were eager to fund the efforts of their brethren to the south.

When John Brown's entourage returned to the States for the final preparation, fund-raising, and planning for the raid on Harpers Ferry, the Mistress became very involved once again as a U.G.R.R. trail conductor. The Mistress was riding a steed back and forth, at times disguised as a jockey, bringing freedom seekers from North Carolina to Virginia and up through the Allegheny Mountains, where the escapees were to set up what would eventually become forts where they would be trained for the future planned attack of slave states to the south after the Harpers Ferry armory was emptied.

While quotes and definite details escape us, it's not too hard to once again profile both John Brown and Mary Ellen Pleasant in a way most academic historians refuse to do. Pleasant was quite active in the Captain's plans for armed insurrection, as well as supportive of the ferocious justice he doled out in "Bleeding Kansas." Like General Tubman, the Mistress clearly had no issue with and supported his means straight up. Also, how could her time in New Orleans and the mentorship with Voodoo Queen Marie Laveau not be discussed? It's simply not realistic to assume they did not explore their common roots. These warriors of many colors and religions shared their stories, views, and spiritual foundations; it's what happens under the banner of fraternity. It also shows yet again that for all the Captain's Evangelical ways, he had a respect for African spirituality, as well as their religions as a potent source of slave revolts from the Caribbean to America. These warriors for freedom were a progressive bunch indeed.

The Mistress was in fairly close proximity to Harpers Ferry during the raid, and upon the routing of the Captain's Immortal Raiders and his capture, it became known that a note from the Mistress was in his possession. With that she took flight. She hid in St. Louis for a while and managed to avoid capture, eventually heading back to San Francisco and her somewhat secret life as the Mistress of the western gateway. While the Mistress mourned the Captain as a martyr, like just about every other warrior abolitionist, her place in history was just getting started.

After Harpers Ferry

Needless to say, one could fill a book with just Mary Ellen Pleasant's life after the Harpers Ferry raid—and people have—but her years in San Francisco had her working again as ringleader of the U.G.R.R. terminus. She continued to use her spy networks and favor among the elites to continue to gain wealth, at one point possessing a fortune in the tens of millions, making her one of the richest women in California.

She used her wealth to fund safe houses more like pioneer villages for the migrants that fled via her tracks to the west. She eventually let it be known that she was a black woman, which didn't go over well in some circles, and public scrutiny would ensue for years. She would go on to challenge the city and state for equal and civil rights at a time it was unheard of to do so. It would then become commonplace for critics to hurl insults at her ranging from being called a madam (there may have been some truth to that) or a whore to "Mammy" as the most common insult in anything published to cast a negative light on her and her efforts. Some of her adversaries would come to find unexpected and mysterious death, to which cries of voodoo and conjure were hurled in her direction, which she gladly accepted. Whatever helped her, she took. Considering one of the buildings she owned and filled with escaped freedom seekers was known as the "hoodoo house," conjure and voodoo were still a big part of her identity.

In 1887 her husband and partner John James would die of diabetes.

Her continued battles for civil rights and knowledge of how the city worked would gain her the title of "Black City Hall," which was cool with her, and she was undoubtedly the "Mother of Civil Rights" for California.

The Mistress sadly lost a great majority of her fortune and spent her last years in poverty. Mary Ellen Pleasant died on January 4, 1904, in San Francisco, and was buried in Tulocay Cemetery in Napa County.

The Elevation of Mistress Mary Ellen Pleasant

The Mistress was mourned by thousands that had her to thank for their homes, jobs, and civil rights. In 1974 the city of San Francisco designated a series of eucalyptus trees that the Mistress herself had planted a memorial in her honor outside of one of her mansions, "The House of Mystery." On the same corner of Octavia and Bush Street as the house, a plaque on the ground that commemorates her is San Francisco's smallest official city park. Author and lecturer Dr. Susheel Bibbs was instrumental in bringing attention to her legacy as well as helping raise money to install a new granite marker on her neglected grave site. The Mistress's grave has been named as a "Network to Freedom" site by the National Park Service. Upon her tombstone it says, "She was a friend of John Brown."

We see in the Mistress a woman of immeasurable courage and generosity, with a profound dedication to the freedom of her people. The Mistress risked her life on countless occasions, from her early days as a clandestine conductor and slave stealer to traveling with the Captain and his Immortal Raiders to leading escapees north on the trails to freedom on horseback. The Mistress forged an entire separate track and her own gateway to freedom in the West. We see a woman in the Mistress who was ahead of her time, fighting for civil rights and in fact helping forge the very title. She was a warrior, skilled in disguise, spying, and manipulation. We have in Mary Ellen Pleasant a mistress of magic, voodoo, and conjure, as she wielded it throughout her life.

Her at times underrated contribution to the U.G.R.R. is unmeasurable but thankfully continues to rise into the light and prominence it deserves.

Her spirit is still as strong and generous as it was in life, and she still has many gifts to share.

When it comes to working with the spirit of the Mistress, we have a warrior from the ranks of General Tubman and Captain Brown. This was a woman who was not just a warrior but a master of espionage, magic, and mystery. She possessed strength, smarts in business, magic, and valor, and successfully combined them all into a formidable concoction.

The skill sets the Mistress applied in life and can still pass on are the stuff of a legendary conjure woman and the Voodoo Queen of California. It's hard to have a better elevated spirit to work with than that.

Working with Mistress Mary Ellen Pleasant

Let's start right off by saying to never, ever refer to her when calling as "Mammy Pleasant"; she was not fond of, and in fact detested, the title. There are indeed many out there who do refer to her in that manner even when trying to do right, but as anyone who knows her legacy as well as her spirit can attest, it's simply not a title that will gain favor from her in any way. Also be aware that when it comes to her portrait, there is only one that is confirmed as her: the one included in this book. For some strange reason, out in the world of meta tagging of internet images there is a perplexing error through which many, even in academia, use various photos for her that are actually of Hawaii's Queen Anna. So when it comes to placing her photograph upon any altar or shrine, be sure to use the one that actually is of Mistress Pleasant. It will go a long way in any sort of tangible conjugations and connection.

Accoutrements for Mistress Pleasant

When it comes to items and tools for the Mistress, it's pretty open to interpretation given the hazy details of her life; but there are traditions that have been regimented into working with her over the years. The Mistress was a conjure woman, a voodoo priestess even and one of lineage via her mother and grandmother, so this opens up a wide selection and array of ways to appease her spirit, as well as what items she will bless when arriving at your shrines or at work toward and for her. So tools and magical trinkets associated with Louisiana voodoo, hoodoo, and conjure will help forge a connection to this unique voodoo queen and conjure woman.

- Her image/photo. The one contained within this book is the only confirmed photo of her.

- A candle. Any color will do. As we know by now, the flame enhances magic. One way to personalize it is to write out the initials she was known to use in correspondence—M.E.P.—on a blank jar candle.

- Flowers of any kind, as well as water. They provide life force, and the Mistress was a lover of flowers and gardening in general.

- Money. Whether in a jar, bowl, or any other way you feel represents a good means to house money on a shrine in order to help manifest more of it, this evokes her history. She was a millionaire conjure woman, so who better to ask for prosperity from within the U.G.R.R. spirit world?

- A chicken foot. Traditional New Orleans magic used these. Placed above doorways, they provide protection via the chicken's ability to "scratch back" at those who send bad juju your way.

- A voodoo doll/poppet. This is another curio and fetish synonymous with New Orleans voodoo. More often than not they are made or bought and personalized and placed in a home for protection. One could use a doll as a representation of her in particular as a house protector.

- Roots, oils, and herbs associated with voodoo and conjure

- An image or replica of a horse. The Mistress rode many a steed, and at one point she passed as a jockey while guiding freedom seekers to safe zones.

- A eucalyptus plant. This is a species of tree that can be grown indoors. Any of the several species for this relative of the myrtle will suffice as a plant of power to her spirit. This is a sacred tree for her. She planted eucalyptus trees herself, some of which are still living in her park in San Francisco.

- Dirt or pebbles from her places of power. If you have been able to make a pilgrimage to either her grave or her park and plaque in San Francisco, then gathering dirt or pebbles from these spots and housing them on your shrine would be a very tangible way to connect with her. If you do get a chance to visit her trees, you can tie a ribbon loosely on any branch, and as you do so on trees she actually planted in life, you can tell her of your devotion and respect, as well as asking for a drop of magic from the Voodoo Queen of California.

- An image of John Brown. Her headstone states she was a friend of John Brown. They were colleagues and are still connected to each other in the afterlife.

Many of these items can be used to create a space for her or to add to one big U.G.R.R. shrine you build to honor the spirits. As stated previous, if there is anything you think would enhance your connection not mentioned here, then enlist it. Allow your intuition and spirit to guide you. However, if possible, procuring a eucalyptus tree or plant and dedicating it to her would be a great way to work with her and develop a conduit to her spirit.

Invoking Mary Ellen "The Mistress" Pleasant

When it comes to invocations to call her forth, this is another place where a great deal of creativity and personal comfort can be utilized, especially considering there is no overtly Christian aspect to her life. Reading her legacy and knowing her tools of power, you could fashion your own way to call her forth. This is not uncommon when it comes to folks working with her spirit. But as an example, a prayer to call to her could be similar in fashion to the one here.

Mary Ellen Pleasant, I call to you and your many powers;

Mistress, Voodoo Queen, conductor, mother of civil rights,

Bless me and my work with the spirits you fought for and freed,

You are the Mistress of the U.G.R.R., you created your own tracks and terminus of freedom, and I ask that your sacred tracks lead to me, my work, and my home.

Gift me with the voodoo magic that is your birthright and the conjure you wielded throughout life and continue to wield in spirit.

Bless me, Mistress, with abundance and prosperity, that I may use to
travel and enhance my work with the spirits of the U.G.R.R.
and share among those I love.

Bless me, Mistress, as I work and stand for the continuation
of your legacy in civil rights.

Beautiful Mistress, I honor you, and I bid you love and Godspeed.

Whether in your home or at her places of power—her grave or city park—with her image and some of the accoutrements mentioned you will be able to call to her tangible spirit, long since elevated and continually revered, to aid you as you exalt her incredible contributions to the U.G.R.R. and all it stood for. She is held in a place of esteem, a conductor and station master, whose very own tracks were a terminus to freedom.

John W. Jones, the Sexton

John W. Jones:
The Sexton

Being a sexton is a sacred duty as an officer of a church or congregation who cares for and chronicles the dead they bury for the church they represent. There are mysteries among sextons that go back to Europe among Anglican denominations, and many a sexton performs certain rites as a verger or layman, especially among the dead they care for and the grounds that house them. John W. Jones is a sacred and tangible spirit among his U.G.R.R. colleagues, the head of the sexton spirits, and someone who had direct connection from his "station" in Elmira, New York, to where his "baggage" would arrive in St. Catharines.

John W. Jones's Early Years

John Jones was born in bondage on June 21, 1817, in Leesburg, Virginia. On June 3, 1844, when his owner was near death and his being sold to another plantation seemed imminent, he and his two half brothers along with two other men fled to the North. Their harrowing 300-mile journey on foot involved fighting off more than one horde of slave hunters. I'll let you figure out what had to be done to win through such a gauntlet. After making it through Delaware and into Pennsylvania, the group arrived in New York State, hungry, scared, and exhausted. They hid out in a barn owned by the Smith family, and Mrs. Smith cared for the freedom seekers till they were ready to move on. John W. Jones was so grateful for her care and aid that when she passed away he sent flowers to her grave every year till he himself entered the afterlife.

He put down roots in Elmira, New York, where he not only worked as a candlemaker, but became one of the most storied sextons of the U.G.R.R. Jones aided over 800 escapees as a station master for the U.G.R.R., many of them staying in his home adjacent to the graveyard he managed or at the grounds of the church he served: Elmira's First Baptist Church. Nearly every single one of his freedom seekers ended up here in my town of St. Catharines. He holds a special place of prominence among many who are around today because of his efforts.

You won't find many books discussing his times spent with Mama Moses, but they did cross tracks, for his station on the U.G.R.R. was uniquely placed between Philadelphia and St. Catharines. By 1850 there were also actual train tracks that could be used. With the aid of white and free black baggage handlers for Northern Central Railway, the "4 o'clock freedom baggage car" was born. Freedom seekers could stow away in baggage cars and arrive in Niagara Falls, New York, exit, and take a short walk across the suspension bridge with a mighty River Jordan below them into Canaan North. Mama Moses and the Sexton did know each other.

He also gifted his "baggage" a unique luxury as they left his station: candles. From the warmth and light they would provide to the prayer and intent behind them, they were multipurpose. These were conjure candles, and some would not be lit till arrival in St. Catharines.

Civil War Sexton and Later Years

When the Civil War began, John W. Jones took a prominent role as the sexton at the Woodlawn Cemetery for the Elmira prison camp. In those years he buried nearly 3,000 captured Confederate soldiers who died from disease or hunger, but did so with an honor that generated immense respect from the Confederate prisoners. He so adhered to his duty as sexton and the mysteries therein that many a dying Confederate beckoned for him, begging that their possessions and last wishes be recorded and placed in safekeeping for their loved ones should a day of peace finally come. His conscientiousness was on an impressive level. He buried the Confederates in lines that represented soldiers at inspection, with their graves clearly marked. At the end of the Civil War when families came to retrieve their loved one's possessions, photos, and last words dictated to the sexton, so many were so impressed with the pattern of graves alongside their brothers and the respect shown that only three were removed to the South for reburial.

John W. Jones died December 26, 1900, and is buried at the Woodlawn National Cemetery, a stone's throw from Mark Twain. His home and renowned station for the U.G.R.R.—The John W. Jones House in Elmira, New York—is a popularly visited site that still stands.

The Elevation of John W. Jones

John W. Jones was a warrior, a station master for the U.G.R.R., and a keeper of the dead, and from his place in the afterlife still honors the dead.

It is worth noting that while John W. Jones is not a Lwa, over the years colleagues discussing John W. Jones do make comparisons to the Haitian Lwa Baron Cimetière. Baron Cimetière is one of three spirits of the dead that are a part of the Baron family housed within Haitian vodou, and he is the one who guards the dead at the cemetery. While there could be a few similarities, John W. Jones is not really the same sort of spirit, nor does he serve the exact same duties or attributes, but for sure there are a few similarities, as is the case for many spirits housed within the U.G.R.R. and various ATRs.

The sexton role was one taken on by many a freedom seeker once they reached the Promised Land. A man named Big George Johnson and his wife Emily, after arrival in St. Catharines from Kentucky via the U.G.R.R., put down roots in Milton, Ontario, about an hour away. Big George became a renowned sexton for St. John's Anglican Church, and Emily became the church organist. A small community of freedom seekers eventually settled with the Johnsons in Milton and called their enclave "Little Kentucky." George's son James would carry on the sexton role for the same church, and his wife Clarissa would become the church organist. All of them now lay buried together in the cemetery of the church they worked for in life. This is but one example of how sextons form an integral part of a community. Nevertheless, many from the U.G.R.R. ranks did not fall under their care, and so sadly their graves were not properly recorded, as with some near the BME Church and Zion Baptist Church in St. Catharines. But, ironically, much of this tradition may not have sprouted had all bodies been accounted for.

Working with the Sexton John W. Jones

There is an entire branch of the U.G.R.R. spirit world of the many sextons that were part of this tradition, but for the purposes of this book we will focus on the one who had the most impact, as well as the one who was immortalized in photography and heads the sexton spirits. John W. Jones's main concern from spirit is the main concern of all who work among this tradition: forgotten souls. He is not a gatekeeper, but he does seek out those plots that are now abandoned or built upon that house his people, and he is better armed to bring his blessings if we show him where they are.

He is an elevated spirit, and can help in his own unique way to guide or comfort those that lay unmarked, as well as serve as a messenger from those forgotten souls to their loved ones and living descendants. He works

Conjure symbol for John W. Jones, the Sexton

tirelessly from his realm, and his work in spirit is as sacred as it was in life. When we come across any abandoned or neglected cemetery, especially those that were the "black" or "negro" cemeteries, as they are called, not only should we build a Cairn and Cross, if possible, but we should leave his mark, his conjure symbol, and call his name.

While he is indeed concerned about his people and the legacy of spirits in the U.G.R.R. family, this man already showed in life that he had compassion even unto those that would enslave him. And so if we come across any abandoned, desecrated, or neglected graveyard of any kind housing any people, white or black, he will still administer his sexton duties. He will be able to help heal and communicate with those spirits, as well as tip his hat to the gatekeeper, for the sexton always knows of the gatekeeper. In fact, sextons still acknowledge that gatekeepers stand guard for the spirits that rest in the grounds they tend to.

Accoutrements for the Sexton

If you are going to revere any aspect of the U.G.R.R. spirit world, John W. Jones should take a place of prominence on any shrine—if only insofar as his image being placed among the others, with a candle lit for him and a glass of water to sustain him. If you want to work with him a bit deeper, you will find he certainly has a unique aspect from his place in spirit.

John W. Jones was a candlemaker and distributed his candles to the passengers that rode into his station, so bear that in mind when working with candles in this tradition, for we have among us one who made them and made them with intent.

When you leave his conjure symbol or create it, any fashion will do—whether printed out, chalked, or laid out in cornmeal or cascarilla. It's up to you and the situation at hand. One can always draw or print out his sigil and place it near or behind his portrait as well, along with the occasional nip of the drink. He is a wonderful spirit, and if you honor him, you will come to find that he is a very attentive, tangible, and loving spirit. His sigil is more potent if it can be laid out beside the sigil for the Cairn and Cross.

Invoking the Sexton

Whenever we enter any cemetery, we can call his name, for he likes to travel from cemetery to cemetery, checking on the dead there and tipping his hat to the gatekeeper. Whenever we erect a Cairn and Cross, know that when we feel the joy of the spirits and acknowledgment from Mama Moses, in the distance the Sexton looks on too with a smile, for we are holding service for what was most sacred to him in life and still in spirit. One night after erecting a Cairn and Cross, in those moments of reflection, you may see him in the shadow bid you a smile and a tip of the hat.

When you come across any house of the dead left in ruin or built upon, in some fashion lay out his sigil or his sigil along with the Cairn and Cross for added power.

In an ideal situation you would leave a jar candle beside it, actually leave it there, and pour out or leave in a small container a good stiff drink of whiskey. Call to him:

John W. Jones, Sexton, station master, hear my call.

There are passengers that need tending to, Sexton, souls that need help.

Bring your strength and light, and help lay their burdens down.

Sexton, I bid you Godspeed!

It may seem odd to suggest leaving his sigil as well as a jar candle at any of these abandoned or neglected locations, but this is a "tag," if you will, a purposeful marker meant to be seen if necessary, and a challenge he has sent forth.

Graveyard Etiquette

Before entering any graveyard for purposes magical or not, always pay the gatekeeper. As you enter the literal threshold, pause. If there is a gate, knock on it three times. If there is nothing that separates the world of the living from that of the dead, then at that threshold acknowledge the gatekeeper. Tell him that you enter in peace and you mean the spirits in that yard no harm. Pay him for his tireless work: a few pennies, nickles, or dimes will do. If you go to enlist the aid of a spirit in that yard, be sure to stop and make a connection with the grave you are about to work with. Always pay the grave from which you take. Whether you leave money yet again, a candle to offer heat, a libation of water and/or alcohol, or all of the above, be sure to pay the grave. As you leave, bid the gatekeeper thanks and farewell. After any working in any graveyard it's best to cleanse yourself, whether with a blessing of Jerusalem oil or Florida Water or through a basic cleansing bath, which could include some of the elements and ingredients from either the rejuvenation or uncrossing baths shared earlier. Things can stick to your spirit, so be sure to cleanse.

Spiritualist William Lloyd Garrison

The Spiritualists

The spiritualist movement was born in the homes, barns, and tracts of land where radical Quakers, freethinkers, and freedom seekers sat down in fraternal assembly and shared their spiritual beliefs, and these tables eventually began to be places of rapping and tapping, manifestation and communication with spirits. The very notion of spirit communication in the manner that became spiritualism was formed between radical Quaker mystics and their belief in a tangible afterlife and the traditions of ancestral veneration among the freedom seekers. Even for those on the tracks to freedom that were Christian, the celebration of one's ancestors was still a major part of African American culture. The formation of spiritualism came about while freedom seekers and their allies demonstrated their ways to one another.

The spiritualist movement took root in the regions of New York State called the "Burned-Over District," which were large sections of central and western New York at the crossroads where numerous tracks, stations, and conductors for the freedom train interacted with one another. These were regions where those freedom seekers that were able spent a bit more time on the properties of "friends." It's where legendary abolitionists, black and white, lived, wrote, and lectured. Storied churches, cemeteries, and Native American lands offered escapees solace and a place of rest. The Burned-Over District was almost a capital region of abolitionism, woman's suffrage, and spiritual awakening.

After many years the foundations of spiritualism took shape and became the celebrated religion we know today, especially in the region where I live on the border of Canada and America's old Burned-Over District. The spiritualists embodied a unique combination of mysticism, heroism, and championship of equality—be it racial, sexual, or religious. This is a profound legacy to have in the Americas: mediums and mystics who championed the U.G.R.R., essentially maintaining much of it. And many of those who practice in the modern age are still connected to their U.G.R.R. colleagues, white and black, who still rap, tap, and whisper from their realm in spirit.

There are some similarities between the courts of U.G.R.R. spirits we call the Spiritualists and the Diviners. For the most part, the Diviners are spirits that were freedom seekers, those who were conjurers, rootworkers, or adherents to their African religions. The Spiritualists are more often the spirits of those who were abolitionists, Quakers, mystics, mediums, and those of European blood and stock. The two courts share a love of divination, and one court may manifest and aid you in connecting to the other, for there were diviners of various methods that were white supporters and are enveloped in the U.G.R.R. spirit world, as well as many black mediums that were central to spiritualist meetings. At times members of both will manifest together, which is a truly wonderful blessing,

For some, this court of spirits will become a sacred and welcomed addition to their magic, conjurations, and work with the spirits of the U.G.R.R. As with the Diviners, that can be a powerful and personal connection with immense blessings and wisdom shared. These are truly beautiful, kind, and powerful spirits.

The notion of a "cross-pollination," in hoodoo in particular, as a shared magical formula and practice influenced by Native American spirituality as well as various European folk magics open for all to claim is misleading at best. Some modern appropriators have even referred to hoodoo as a cake recipe, saying that Europeans added to the mix and therefore can claim a place at the table where said cake is served. The reality is that, while there were elements of Native American mythology and iconography added to hoodoo conjurations and formula, as well as fragments of European folk magic and witchcraft incorporated into elements of sorcery—of which most was gleaned by those who were stationed in the big house for the French Catholic slave masters—it was assembled solely by the African Americans and what they had to do in order to add to their evolving mysticism. Straight up it was their invention and ingenuity.

In some ATRs in the Americas, especially in Brazil, a branch that grew out of the spiritualist tree known as spiritism founded by Frenchman Allan Kardec is heavily practiced. This aspect is attractive to many who immerse themselves in those traditions, because once again the synergy was easily adapted from the African traditions of ancestor veneration and the trance state. However, that is a part of another culture's spirituality, at least the way Brazilians have assimilated spiritism into their fold, as well as the Espiritismo in Cuba and Puerto Rico. The Spiritualists of the U.G.R.R. are North America's mediums with roots nourished in antislavery and the battle against its horrendous legacy.

Working with the Spiritualists of the U.G.R.R.

There are a few ways to connect to and work with the Spiritualists. Much like with the Diviners and Healers, it will eventually be based upon your own formula and innovation once you make an established connection. These are tangible spirits, who in life were immersed in contact with the spirit world, and they manifest routinely from the afterlife to those that can hear, see, and feel their presence. There are members of the Spiritualists that are named and known, but there are also lesser known, unnamed spirits within the court. These tend to be Quaker spirits who were practitioners, conductors, or ones who opened their homes as stations for the U.G.R.R. To this day there are still Quaker spiritualists whose contributions to aiding and abetting runaways is not set down or captured within the annals of history. Localized oral histories will at times reveal some, but for the most part, the contributions of these unnamed are lost to the seas of time. There are also within this court those who were mediums, again some immortalized in history as renowned seers but also ardent abolitionists and U.G.R.R. supporters, but others who had a lower profile. The latter did their work in less public venues and remote homesteads, but they too will manifest to a willing summoner. Who presents themselves and aids in your conjures will depend on what aspect of spirit work you approach them with. With a responsible effort toward protection—and thankfully the U.G.R.R. spirit world is one of interconnectedness and elevation—there is very little danger of any kind to invoking the Spiritualists.

One can utilize many ways to house a place or create a space for the Spiritualists. Some of you reading this will in fact be spiritualists yourselves and will know exactly how to connect with these spirits within your system, but there are some tested and true ways to invoke them through a familiar formula that will enhance your connection to the U.G.R.R. spirit world as a whole.

For an altar or shrine for the Spiritualists, it is best to follow the steps to cleanse and sanctify the area where the shrine will go, assuming it will not be among the other tools and portraits you have already gathered and assembled for a combined space for the U.G.R.R. spirits.

Spiritualist Tools of Power and Accoutrements

- A human skull. This can be a replica, of course. The skull is a great tool to help focus on the dead, as well as an amplifier and conduit to spirit. This can be especially useful when conducting a service or séance with them.

- A candle. This can be any kind of candle, but best white for the purity and positivity it emits when illuminated, at least at first. Eventually and for some any color could be used and justified. It depends on one's skill as a summoner or medium. The candle's flame will of course also help sustain the visit from spirit.

- An image of the Freedom Seeker. Ras is a wonderful spirit and protector, as well as a sign to the spirit world we intend to work with them. He can help you connect to the Spiritualists court, as we will see soon.

- The tools of séance and mediumship. These can be from a vast array of items associated with these practices as well as the era of spiritualism you are planning to honor. These include the séance trumpet, pads for automatic writing, a crystal ball, or crystals in general. A Herkimer diamond can be wonderful, as a gem from the region where the movement was born. Other possible options are a scrying mirror, pendulum, or spirit board and planchette. When it comes to the spirit board—best known as a Ouija board—they do carry a stigma about them, but with a sensible approach and intent, there really is little difference between a spirit board and a pendulum. The same principles are involved.

- Dolls/effigies. These can portray Quakers, pioneers of the era, and people of European descent. These are much like effigies of the Followers, only the dolls are of a different ethnicity.

- Photos. There are many well-known spiritualists that were also abolitionists and U.G.R.R. supporters; the entire movement was wrought with antislavery support from top to bottom on a very proactive level. Many of these kind mystics have been immortalized in photography. We can adorn our shrines with their images, or place them at a space where we intend to hold a service. This is another unique aspect of certain sections of the U.G.R.R. spirit world: that their faces live on and their photos can add a palpable bump to connecting with their spirits. Following are a few of the spiritualists, mediums, and abolitionists involved in the movement for whom we have photos:

Amy and Isaac Post. Both wife and husband were abolitionists and members of the radical Hicksite Quaker sect.

Cora L. V. Scott. This renowned pre–Civil War medium, as well as abolitionist, was also known for her alluring beauty.

Thomas Garrett. One of the most celebrated abolitionists and U.G.R.R. station masters, he was a close friend to Harriet Tubman. He was a leader in the U.G.R.R. and there was no secret about it. He was also an adherent to spiritualism and attended countless meetings along with many of his U.G.R.R. and abolitionist colleagues.

William Lloyd Garrison. This renowned abolitionist and U.G.R.R. supporter on many levels was a regular attendee at spiritualist meetings.

Paschal Beverly Randolph. A free man of mixed race and a spiritualist medium in the years prior to the Civil War, he was involved in the abolitionist movement, as well as being a doctor, occultist, and founder of the first Rosicrucian Order in the United States. Randolph is an underrated figure in the American occult who is worth learning more about, and he strikes a good photo for your potential shrine.

- Flowers in water. Any kind will be good for their life force and aroma. However, if sunflowers are ever available these would be great to adorn any space for the Spiritualists as well as any U.G.R.R. shrine. The sunflower itself is associated with the American Spiritualist Church, for its being native to North America and its connection to the sun. A motto of one of the branches of the American Spiritualist Church is: "As the sunflower turns its face to the light of the sun, so Spiritualism turns the face of humanity to the light of the truth."

- A glass of water. For water is the essence of life.

- Images and symbols associated with the Quaker faith, such as the eight-pointed red-and-black star, or spiritualist movement, like the sunflower.

- Quilt code images. The quilt codes were utilized on some Quaker properties, and their symbolism is at times a cross between African American and Quaker quilting traditions.

A Service and Séance with the Spiritualist Court

To some, what I am about to suggest—a "meeting" and séance with Spiritualist court—may sound kind of crazy, but nothing offered in these pages has not been done by many over many years with healthy success and manifestation. Spiritualism is a reflection of the foundations of conjure here in the northeastern United States and Southern Ontario. It is a part of the legacy that is still solid and continues to be practiced to this day. From eastern Ohio to northern Pennsylvania, western New York, and Southern Ontario, the elements of séance and spirit communication make up a part of how conjure is practiced. Even in areas of western New York with a high African American population, you will find this form of work to be common; channeling and mediumship are a legacy in the region for both blacks and whites. With the Lily Dale spiritualist community of New York being an ever-present force in the region, African, Latin, European, and to an extent Native Americans—of which there are large nations on both sides of the border—interact, learn, and share with one another in numerous colorful ways. The cross-pollination and methods of the beloved U.G.R.R. mystics are still being forged. Because strong and sound mediumship roots were planted on the last stretches of the U.G.R.R., it's what grows in my front yard. Communication with spirit is a cornerstone for the conjure of the Northeast. If you follow the procedure in these pages and do so with your own added experimentation, you will be honing your own mediumship and intuition skills, albeit in ways specific to U.G.R.R. conjure and the spirit world of Mama Moses.

While much of the work in these pages is good for a solitary practitioner, the séance and service with the Spiritualists is best done with at least two people, unless of course you are already comfortable with what will assuredly become raps, taps, and whispers in time.

MATERIALS AND TOOLS

- White candles. These can be of any kind, but there should be at least three for the heat and illumination they provide.

- Glasses of water. For a séance with the spirits there should be at least three to provide life force and quench the thirst for each "family" of the spirits that may arrive: the Spiritualists, the Mediums, and the Freedom Seekers.

- Flowers of any kind in water for their life force and aroma, sunflowers of course being optimal if possible.

- A food offering. This can be aromatic fruits, which will give off a scent that will attract a visit. A loaf of whole bread that will be broken in half will also act as aromatic attraction as well as sustenance. *Optional:* Another traditional offering of sustenance for séance in some traditions is a hardy and flavorful warm soup.

- An image of Ras the Freedom Seeker. He acts as a guide for our intent toward the spirits we want to connect with.

- An image or version of the Cairn and Cross sigil.

- Images or chalked/drawn out versions of any of the quilt codes. These not only act as an attractor and sign of intent, but they bring protection as well.

- A human skull. This can be a replica, of course.

It should go without saying, but just to be clear: never conduct a séance when intoxicated.

STEPS OF THE SERVICE

- As the first step, make an effort to turn off mobile devices, etc.

- Arrange a table with the offerings, accoutrements, sigils, and flowers. This could be on a separate but close location to the séance table.

- When placing the food and water offerings, it's good to enlist the "cross motion" we have used for our altars or another one that suits you, like a pentagram. Making this motion and then passing the offering through the symbol before setting it down signifies it's for those in the realm of spirit.

- Light the candles, saying:

  We offer illumination and warmth for the spirits.

- Turn off all extraneous lights if possible.

- Break the loaf of bread in two and recite:

  We offer this sacrifice for the spirits.

- Assemble and sit around the table.

At this point it is recommended for the participants to join hands, as well as have one person in particular chosen to recite the incantations and intent throughout. This would normally be a person who is a medium or channel. However, for these works this task can be taken on by anyone willing, thereby allowing a possible channel present to be free to work their craft. After a few séances of this nature, certain folks will realize they have the calling, which is a great sign and step toward building stronger relationship for communication with spirit. I will call the speaker the medium in the following steps.

All participants should close their eyes, other than the medium if recitation is needed via written word.

- The medium begins with opening calls and prayers:

  We gather in a circle of friends, as a circle of friends.
  It is friends from spirit we wish to reach.

May our collective good and kind souls be recognized from spirit, so sayeth us.

(Everyone repeats: "So sayeth us.")

We praise the almighty deity, the source of all that is born,
and to whom we shall all return in death, praise be.

(Everyone repeats: "Praise be.")

We honor the Native lands we sit upon, may their spirits be with their relations, and may this service have their blessing.

It is our collective will that only good and kind spirits be in our presence, so sayeth us.

(Everyone repeats: "So sayeth us.")

It is our collective will that any spirit that is hateful or deceiving shall not enter our circle of friends, nor afflict our service for the spirits, so sayeth us.

(Everyone repeats: "So sayeth us.")

We are gathered together to honor and call to the spirits of the U.G.R.R.

We are gathered to call to those kind friends in spirit.

We honor those spirits that walked the roads less traveled.

We honor those that housed the travelers.

We honor those who maintained the roads less traveled.

And we honor those brave souls that guided them along the tracks and trails of freedom, and we offer those trails to the living for those that need them on this night.

Let our circle of friends be a station house for the spirits.

- Instruct the people at the table to now unlock their hands, with eyes still closed, and place their hands upon the table surface in front of them.

- Let a moment or two pass by in silence, then continue:

Freedom Seeker, runner of the U.G.R.R., Ras, kind spirit and guide, Freedom Seeker, guide and messenger of your realm, manifest among us; see our collective good.

Take strength among this circle of friends.

Take warmth.

Quench thirst.

Ferry for us messages to and fro.

Ferry for us, Freedom Seeker, we wish you Godspeed.

- Let a moment or two pass by in silence, then continue:

We call to those who sat in a circle as friends,

to the Mediums,

to the Spiritualists,

to the Freedom Seekers,

join us in assembly.

- Let a moment or two pass by in silence, then continue:

Spiritualists in the afterlife, join our assembly, encircle our meeting in protection, sit among us now in death as you did in life.
We bid you welcome.

- Let a moment or two pass by in silence, then continue:

Thomas Garrett, kind friend of Mama Moses,

you who funneled so many to freedom,

you who attended meetings such as ours,

let the word be heard that a circle of friends is in meeting.

Let the spirits of the U.G.R.R. know we honor them with love and respect.

Take a seat of prominence among us, and join our meeting.

We honor you, Thomas Garrett, and we bid you welcome.

- Let a moment or two pass by in silence, then continue:

    Mediums join us at our table as you did in life.

    Let us feel your spirit course through our circle.

    We bid you welcome.

- Let a moment or two pass by in silence, then continue:

    Use our circle and manifest among us.

    Speak to us as the spirits did for you.

    Join us in the ballet of life and death,

    so sayeth us.

    (All repeat: "So sayeth us.")

    Join our hands, Mediums. Bring blessings from the spirits.

    Take strength from our circle.

    Take warmth.

    Quench thirst.

    Feel love.

- Let a moment or two pass by in silence, then continue:

    We hold this service, kind spirits, in your honor.

    We complete the circle and give you the voice you once sought from spirit.

    Speak to us so that we can hear your whisper.

- Let a moment or two pass by in silence, then continue:

    Mediums in the afterlife, gift us with a message.

    Let us hear you as a collective,

    or gift us in private that which we need to see or hear.

- Let a moment or two pass by in silence, then continue:

  *Mediums, if there are messages from the spirits of the U.G.R.R.,
  let us hear them.*

  Let them know who we are and that we honor them.

- Let a moment or two pass by in silence, then continue:

  Spiritualists and Mediums, reveal to us your face.

  Reveal to us your essence.

  How shall we know you again?

  Reveal to us that which would be familiar, for we wish to call you friend.

  Let us recognize you as friends in the future.

  Seek one who shall speak for you.

  Share with the living.

- Allow for someone to potentially speak for spirit.

- Let a moment or two pass by in silence, then continue:

  We pray that you kind spirits always be illuminated by your god.

  We pray that you kind spirits continue to be at peace in your realm.

  *You are blessed kind spirits, for you gather among your fellow kind souls;
  you continue to be remembered.*

  We invite you to continue to call us friends.

- Let a moment or two pass by in silence, then continue:

  Let us close this door between the living and the dead.

  Let us bid you farewell until we meet again.

Gather strength from our circle so that you may remain strong in your realm.

Gather heat so that you may remain warm in your realm.

Quench your thirst.

Gather love, and know you are loved, ye kind spirits.

- Let a moment or two pass by in silence, then continue:

This meeting has concluded. Return to your realm in love.

We thank you, until next we call again spirits,

Godspeed!

(All repeat: "Godspeed!")

Let a moment or two pass by in silence, then ask everyone to open their eyes.

This can be a great group working to explore or experiment with. Provided you take the steps to ensure some responsible tactics, as well as add to any of this formula for those already immersed in similar practices, it can be a rewarding exercise and will allow for manifestation from spirit to take place in any number of ways. When the instructions say, "let a moment or two pass by in silence," this is a fluid suggestion based on how your ritual transpires. This is a frame and suggestion to start from in conducting a séance as a service for the spirits, and by doing so makes this a voodoo as well, similar to the other group workings and rituals.

The séance session with and for the spirits of the U.G.R.R., and in particular for the Spiritualists court, can be a great working to do whenever possible, especially when you are in the company of friends or a community that is open to exploration. Much like with the Marriage of the Bride and Groom or erecting the Cairn and Cross and the Baptism, these are workings that can be done at open or inclusive celebrations or holidays as they pertain to some who follow the wheel of the year. For those times that this working is shared or done among several attendees, it is fine for folks to sit on the perimeter, being silent and acting as extra energy. Also a person skilled in channeling can roam that very perimeter with those who sit as observers and share what comes to them during the suggested moments of silence for exchange.

I realize that this working can take some considerable preparations and planning, but the results can be well worth it. I hope you can share this with others, and bring more strength, warmth, and love to the spirits of the U.G.R.R. and the blessings they have to give, allowing them to rap, tap, and whisper to the living. The Spiritualists still hold meetings and sessions in their spirit world, and we do them honor and service by allowing them to commune with us in the living, in fraternity as friends.

The Baptism: Walking with General Tubman across the River Jordan

As we have come to learn, the family of spirits within the U.G.R.R. and its mysteries are a colorful group. From the Followers who can branch off into the Diviners and Healers to the Spiritualists and Mediums, they are as unique an array in spirit as they were in life. Despite what each family or court of spirits represents, they all had a life filled with devotion toward a deity . . . or two. But our spirits of the U.G.R.R. not only worshipped the divine, they also invoked it, called it down, walked and talked alongside it, taking instructions and following through. Much like a spiritualist meeting and the wedding for the Lovers, we can hold a baptism for and with them, and doing so allows us to receive holy blessings from those that can bestow them, similar to working with them in a ritual bath or wash.

Now for those who may get a bit uncomfortable with baptisms and what they represent, let me share that baptism is truly an ancient and sacred act and predates the Christianity that adopted it. Baptism was so important that even Jesus Christ sought one from John the Baptist. No faith owns the baptismal act; it just varies what one is baptized for. There are indeed many forms of baptism, and many of the faiths that contribute to the quilt that is the U.G.R.R. spirit world enlisted them. For some this

Cairn and Cross conjure symbol known as the General Tubman

was done indoors in church, for others in a river, pond, or swamp. Many of the U.G.R.R. spirits in the court of the Followers were Baptists, faith healers, as well as conjurers, all of whom created their own versions of what a baptism is: a cleansing, a renewal, a vow, a healing, and a burden lifted. For our work with the spirits of the U.G.R.R., we baptize each other—human and spirit, together hand in hand.

The spirits we work with have the capacity to heal from their realm, especially the Healers. Much like the joy our meeting with the Spiritualists can bring for those very spirits that once spoke to the dead and now speak to us, the Healers will be overjoyed to dance in the ballet between the living and the dead as we honor their ways. There are of course many who have gone on to the embrace of their god and the angels, but many have chosen to stay and work among the living with their U.G.R.R. friends and colleagues in spirit. By invoking those who had a great love of the act of a baptismal cleansing, we give them strength while we honor them. If we work with spirits that were Diviners to help divine and spirits of Mediums who help us channel, then inviting those who not only had love and devotion toward baptisms but were faith healers in life to now do so from the afterlife is yet again what is unique about this spirit world.

But the ritual here is a unique baptism unto a purpose: walking many metaphorical miles to our freedom, crossing the metaphorical River Jordan, and being cleansed at the end of our journey. We will invoke Mama Moses in her guise as General Tubman, so she will be present for this working. She will inspire us to emancipation from that which burdens us, and on her tracks we will walk with her. Upon our journey's end as we cross the River Jordan, the Healers will baptize us in the name of freedom.

This ritual, although it can be done solo, is best with a group of people; and when done as such with the formula offered, it becomes a voodoo and one uniquely North American, celebrating the legacy of the U.G.R.R.

This voodoo is a cross between three versions that have been shared at times in slightly different ways, combining elements of the ones facilitated by me, Orion Foxwood, and Baba Ted Jauw and Kate Jauw. We have all done them together in different combinations and at different locations in both Canada and the United States.

The conjure symbol for this working is the Cairn and Cross, but it is a variant called The General Tubman.

The General Tubman was conceived by Baba Ted Jauw, and in doing so he has acted in the way I have been encouraging throughout the book: expanding upon the paradigm that this spirit world offers. Maintain the sacredness, maintain the foundations of what the U.G.R.R. spirit world offers, but feel into it and allow it to expand and grow to encompass your own experiences with it. By doing so, we empower the very spirit world we draw from and exalt. The General Tubman obviously houses other mysteries within the Cairn and Cross and its symbolism.

- We see the Cairn and Cross conjure symbol with the Star of David, the square and compass/Marassa as the foundation, and the skeleton with many of the same mysteries. Yet it opens up to a different door and mystery contained within the same spirit world: travel and life, as opposed to a commemoration of death.

- We see the Drinking Gourd, the Cup of Conjure, but in this case a different mystery is illuminated. In Baba Ted's words: "This is the drinking gourd on your left that points you to the North Star across the river. There is no evidence that this symbol was a 'dipper.' African dippers were long and slender. In Yoruba cosmology, the Ija (Sopera) or drinking gourd is the carrier of the Orisa, and Tubman carried a drinking gourd that was said to be a charm or what is called carrier magic. It also is a symbol of time running out. This is the left hand of protection and whatever medicine she carried."

- We see the crescent moon and star. In Baba's words: "The waning crescent is a sign of time running out, but it also symbolizes a crescent machete or sword of protection. With the star, it represents the Masonic ideals of 'parabola' or focus, a maritime sailing principle of nighttime navigation. This is the Right Hand of Guidance and represents General Moses as a seer and visionary."

- We see that the cross is not placed within the cairn, allowing life to flow forth. As it exits the cairn, it takes the guise of a snake with its head at the top, for we will shed our skin and be renewed upon our journey's end as we ride the great snake. In Haitian vodou that is Damballa; in American voodoo it is Grandfather Rattlesnake.

- Upon the sacred serpent we see the train tracks on the vertical beam of the cross, the mode of travel, the metaphorical tracks to freedom.

- We see at the crossroads of the cross itself the machete: our sacred blade for the conjurations of this spirit world. As well it illuminates the warrior aspect of General Tubman and what the machete stands for: revolution and fighting for our freedom.

- The X's across the crossbeam of the cross are what you will choose to do at a the crossroads of any journey to freedom: Fight? Freeze? Flee? You will decide when you walk the sigil, but another snake waits and offers to alleviate that which burdens you, encouraging you to shed your skin.

Armed with the different mysteries of the General Tubman sigil overlaid upon the doorway that is the Cairn and Cross, you can now lay it out to be walked for the baptismal that awaits.

I again will describe this voodoo as one done by a group of people, much like the other voodoos shared, as one that can be done indoors or out, at any open ritual or celebration at any time during the wheel of the year.

INGREDIENTS AND MATERIALS

It is best to set up an altar for the baptism, whether indoors or out, off to the side which could contain any of the following items:

- An image of Mama Moses

- The sigil for the Cairn and Cross

- A Bible and cross to appease the spirits that were faith healers or clergy

- Candles. Any color or many colors are fine, but at least three jar candles on the altar would be ideal for heat and illumination.

- Three glasses of water

- Flowers of any kind in water, purchased or picked.

- Effigies/dolls. These could be any dolls or effigy statues as described for the Followers. However, these dolls or effigies do not have to be ones that portray people of color, as many faith healers that were supporters of the U.G.R.R. as well as some spiritualists who enlisted the laying of hands were white. There are many variations of sewn or mass-produced dollies that portray Quakers or people from the era we draw from. But some effigies on the altar will help it become that much more of an attractive and active portal to the spirits.

- An image of Ras the freedom Seeker

Gather the following items for the baptism:

- A large tote/container. This will be filled with water, and the larger, the better, whether indoors or out. It should be big enough for a person to stand in.

- Chalk, cascarilla, or any way to mark the General Tubman sigil for this voodoo. This can be done even by using masking tape or any way that you can create the conjure symbol.

- A small taper candle of any color for each person in attendance.

- A machete would be good to have. In fact, if there were two and you could lay the sigil out large enough, you could put the two machetes where they are drawn, or just the one. Still draw out the shapes but place the actual blade(s) on top. (Feed the machete(s) first if you do, as well as after.)

- Herbs. This is open to interpretation, so use whatever herbs represent to you ones that are for healing and cleansing. Collect enough to sprinkle into the container of water, whether from your kitchen cupboard or magical shelves.

- Florida Water/Hoyt's Cologne. Either is good to add to the infusion of water.

- Local herbs/grasses/flowers. Once again, let spirit guide you if you are not well versed in what grows in your area that has healing properties. But it is good to remember that every single living plant, herb or grass, as long as it's not poisonous, has a healing quintessence to it of some sort. Even the poisonous ones can heal, but let's leave those out of this concoction unless you are schooled in such matters. Even if it's the dead of winter in the north, you will be able to retrieve tree foliage or grasses from below the snow, so basically harvest anything or a few things that are from your power of place and dwelling. Grab a few pinches to put into the water.

- Change. This can be anything from a few pennies, dimes, etc., as they will be going into the water to invoke future prosperity.

The container of water is essentially similar in nature to the both the rejuvenation and uncrossing baths, but serving as more of a symbolic "sacred river of holy water."

PREPARATIONS

It does not matter how large you lay out the General Tubman Cairn and Cross, but if you have the space indoors or out, go big. It will be worth it, and it's a great exercise to lay out a sigil on a large scale. At the very least, for this to be effective it should be about seven feet in length. I have been part of this ritual where the sigil was over twenty feet long.

- Begin by cleansing and cleaning the ground surface, both inside or outdoors. Florida Water works great to cleanse and change the vibration of your working area.

- Lay out the General Tubman conjure symbol in whatever medium you have chosen, preferably before the others arrive if there will be several attendees, using the same mechanisms and intent as drawing out a smaller one.

- Fill your container/tote with water and some or all of the ingredients mentioned, and place it a few feet past the head of the General Tubman sigil, above the Star of David.

- You can light up and empower the altar ahead of time alone or with whomever is facilitating this voodoo with you, or do that with the attendees present to further connect everyone involved. It's a variable that you will decide on based on circumstances.

- As a starter, you can also cast sacred space ahead of time or at the beginning of the working in a manner that you are comfortable with; the energies will be harmonious regardless.

You will want to have at least two other folks assisting in the Baptism. One or two will be stationed at the container of water to channel the Healers. They will be the ones that will be blessing the people that have walked the sigil and arrive at the cleansing waters, which will be the "River Jordan" that one finally crosses to freedom. There should also be a person or guide to greet them after they exit the "river" to welcome and motion them back to the surrounding group, handing them a taper candle for later.

Welcome those in attendance, explaining that they will have the opportunity to walk toward their freedom, leaving behind that which burdens them by the grace of Mama Moses and the spirits of the U.G.R.R.

Explain what will be happening in walking the conjure symbol of the Cairn and Cross in its aspect as the General Tubman. This is a good time to, either with prepared notes or committed to memory, explain the mysteries of the Cairn and Cross and its symbolism at least on a basic level. Then you can further explain the difference and basic outline of the General Tubman before you.

Tell folks to focus on what burdens them, whether it is emotional, spiritual, or physical. Inform them that as they walk the sigil slowly, starting at the Cairn, they will pause at the crossroads where the machetes are placed or drawn, and at that point each person is to leave their burden behind, severed by the machetes wielded by General Tubman.

They will then continue on their last few steps exiting the sigil and step into the container of water (this is a good time to tell folks to remove their shoes and socks!) to be baptized and renewed in the name of freedom.

- Call forth to Mama Moses:

General Tubman, General Tubman, General Tubman! Mama Moses, we call to you and your Followers, to the Healers, to the Spiritualists, to those in your court who heal and cleanse, bless and baptize. Guide us on a journey to freedom, help us lay a burden down. Praise be to you, Mama Moses, and your Followers. Hail General Tubman!

(Everyone can repeat: "Hail General Tubman!")

- Before the first person begins to walk the sigil slowly, possibly have everyone in attendance join in a song to be maintained throughout this phase. In this case the most effective song is Baba Ted Jauw's contribution: the spiritual "Down to the River to Pray."

Each person who steps onto the General Tubman conjure symbol will indeed be transformed by the end of the journey. With emphasis on the pause at the crossroads and machetes, while everyone is in unison and song it will have impact. The presence of General Tubman will be felt, and each person will leave that burden behind, the snake taking it away to the left. At the very least, a person will have had a chance to really identify what it is that is weighing them down, and that will make letting it go in the near future that much more tangible. Regardless, it is rare that a person does not even for a short while feel the burden lifted and the blessing of General Tubman in those moments. It's a personal journey and one that can bring on emotion.

As each person exits the sigil, they enter into the "River Jordan" to receive their baptism of freedom by stepping into the water. (This is a preferred time to motion for the next individual to begin walking the cross.) This is when the person or persons at the container charged with administering the baptism and cleansing will do their work.

The person at the water will want to allow themselves to be in the moment, cognizant that they are in a manner depending for their comfort on the ones channeling the Healers or any of the U.G.R.R. spirits that are attracted to the call, following General Tubman to the rite.

If you are the one administering the baptism and cleansing, you begin by laying your hands on the attendee's feet for just a moment, and allow spirit to flow thorough you, filled with love and compassion for the attendee who has just faced and fled bondage and now needs cleansing. Bring your hands out of the water and transfer the baptismal water's energy to their hands, heart, and head, again allowing spirit to flow through you. This work for each person present will be your own personal journey and service with the spirits.

Words you could share upon completion are: "You are baptized in the name of freedom, god bless and Godspeed," or you can remain silent—you will decide.

Once everyone has completed the walk of freedom, been baptized at the end, and been handed their taper candle, each person facilitating the baptismal should in turn be provided with the same ceremony while the attendees still sing. Give each other a cleanse, with special emphasis on those who cleansed and baptized each attendee, helping them ground.

- Bring the singing to a close.

- Remind everyone that they have and will be blessed by the spirits, and in particular Mama Moses as General Tubman.

- Remind them that they walked with a heavy burden, and by the grace of the spirits have laid that burden down and been baptized and cleansed in honor of their freedom.

- Then have everyone light their taper candles, either off one another or from a person that provides the light or both.

As everyone stands in the glow of the candles, remind them that they have been illuminated, they possess light and no longer darkness, and their light will continue to shine on. This will be a beautiful sight, and the blessings and presence of Mama Moses will be felt.

- While the candles are still lit with each person, this is a good time to end the working.

- Call out loud:

We thank Mama Moses. General Tubman, we praise you with love and gratitude. To the Followers, Healers, and spirits of the U.G.R.R., we thank you and bid you Godspeed. Hail General Tubman!

(Everyone repeats: "Hail General Tubman!")

After a few moments, people can extinguish their candle to take back home with them and relight as a reminder and token of their baptism and walking with General Tubman across the River Jordan. This is a good time to approach the altar and express extra gratitude while there will still surely be presence of spirit. This is a good moment to absorb the working and voodoo you shared, the blessings you have invoked, and the spirits you have provided service with. You are blessed.

If you had previously used some other form of casting a sacred space at the beginning, this would be the time you can use your methods to fully close down what you cast.

Nameless quilter. (Library of Congress, Jack Delano photograph)

The Quilt Codes
of Freedom

When it comes to U.G.R.R. history, much has been lost because it was not shared by those who understood much of its secretive ways. Many still feared a reprisal long after emancipation—and rightly so. Also many who knew the secrets of the trails—especially from a black perspective—didn't think it was anyone else's business. Nobody knew that the U.G.R.R. would become a celebrated legacy long after the fact.

So the existence and scope of secret messages coded in quilts are a topic of debate. However, it is widely believed that a series of codes were sewn on quilts by both those on the U.G.R.R. tracks—freedom seekers, Quaker "conductors," and "station masters"—and those on plantations to distribute secret news of impending escapes. Routes, news, supplies needed, etc., were encoded in sewn patterns that could be hung over porches and on clotheslines, and displayed in various other ways for the eyes of those who needed them under the nose of those who did not. As someone who has been immersed in U.G.R.R. lore and magic for a long time, I certainly have an opinion on the matter.

The quilt codes of freedom are where historical research and oral history collide. Several black churches in both Canada and the United States have various quilts showing various codes hung as decor and for cultural/historical purposes. That goes for more than one U.G.R.R. museum as well. Numerous statuary and commemorative installations incorporate quilt code–inspired symbolism. In fact, for decades some of these symbols have been used for spiritual and magical purposes as well—right into this modern era, as handed down through the oral traditions that are a paramount part of African American culture and U.G.R.R. lore.

Oral history is the source of much of what we know of the U.G.R.R., especially what is passed down among tight-knit circles, families, and spiritual congregations. Where Quaker mystics and freedom seekers formed a fraternity and passed on codes, ways, and means meant only for those "friends" in the know is where uncomfortable elements come into play for some arms of historical research, for this is where Spiritualism can be found: rapping and tapping, séances, and the like—elements of spiritual practice that are frowned upon still. When it comes to the legacy they have to pass on as far as the U.G.R.R., it is here that accusations of superstition and fantasy begin to be hurled. But if I have learned one thing in my years in the homes and circles of freedom seeker descendants listening to their oral traditions, it is that I will not be one who will challenge their narrative—far from it. I consider myself lucky to be trusted with these narratives, and if they exist from Alabama and the Carolinas right up into parts of Ohio, Pennsylvania, and Ontario, I'm not about to question any of it. And I am not alone in this. A few curators of U.G.R.R. collections maintain the fabric of oral tradition, displaying quilts, symbols, and curios that were undoubtedly a part of the freedom train but not celebrated aspects because they shed light upon an African spiritual foundation. Christian-based entities, white and black, tend to shoot down, refute, and denounce as often as possible.

Were quilt codes used across all U.G.R.R. routes and safe houses? Of course not. But they were most certainly employed regionally at certain plantations and among certain communities where news and mysteries were shared. The notion that secret codes were too complicated to be effective—that it would have been hard for the freedom seekers and their supporters to distribute such a code in the first place—is also ignoring the reality of secret societies and how they carried over from Africa despite all the odds stacked against them. The place of the secret society in African religions conjures discomfort in certain Christian minds, for this draws a line on a very tangible level to voodoo, Lukumí, and conjure surviving to this day. With that existing foundation quilt codes could easily be created and fostered by those held in bondage and then shared with those they knew they could trust, white or black. This notion of a quilt code system and those who used them makes more sense than the opposite put forward by certain branches of white America that the codes are their legacy as opposed to a vital part of the African American experience.

In the 1990s Dr. Gladys-Marie Fry, a black Americana historian and folklorist, brought more light to the subject, as well as African American quilter Ozella McDaniel Williams, who shared her family's generations-old quilt code. Their popular books forced the hand of history to reevaluate the quilt codes and their place in U.G.R.R. history, even if this area is still scrutinized.

Using the Quilt Code Symbols

The quilt codes are powerful sigils in and of themselves and have been used as such for decades. They have been employed for many years for a variety of magic, art, and invocation purposes, ranging from protection work to conjuration, as well officially placed upon sacred sites that in some instances house the graves of unknown and unnamed freedom seekers. Every person I know who works with the U.G.R.R. spirit world utilizes some of the quilt code symbols on altars, on walls, or above doorways. People with the skill set to do so have created actual quilts to adorn homes and temples depicting some of the better-known quilt codes or ones they have fashioned themselves in homage. We don't need to know to what extent exactly the quilt codes were used on the tracks of freedom to tap into their power. They have been immortalized and elevated in an oral tradition that spans a continent. For decades after the U.G.R.R. tracks ceased to be used, they have been spiritual fetishes: magic sewn into being to honor those who fought for their freedom as well as those who helped the freedom train run. These symbols from the quilt codes I share here will lend a hand in forming a potent connection to the spirits of the U.G.R.R. and the sacred magic they have to share.

Shoofly

This is a beneficial sigil. It was used in quilts to signify a guide, a trusted person white or black who could lead escapees to the next safe location. The Shoofly can be drawn out in chalk or cascarilla on any surface before certain conjurations as an extra push for gaining the trust of any of the U.G.R.R. spirits, but most assuredly the Followers and Spiritualists. It can be used as a marker on the outside of your home to signify to traveling spirits that your house, altar, and work are good and trusted and will invoke a visit. It is also a great symbol to place in any fashion above windows or doorways. There really is no end as to how many creative ways the Shoofly can be applied in your U.G.R.R. conjure. As I shared with the first conjure in the book for working with the North Star, if you are working with and guiding the U.G.R.R. spirits, you are a shoofly yourself.

Log Cabin

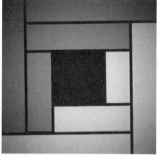

The Log Cabin is also a great marker to spirits of the U.G.R.R who wander or seek solace from shrine to shrine. While it was used in the quilt codes, it was also drawn out on the floor or porch to indicate that the person, regardless of whether white or black, was safe to talk to and exchange information with. This is a great sigil to lay out in chalk or cascarilla at the beginning of any U.G.R.R. spirit summoning. It is also a great symbol to place outdoors on your home, above any window, or directly on any altar or shrine.

North Star

This sigil tells spirits that you and your work are blessed by the magical light of the guiding star of freedom. While some of the sigils in this book utilize the mystery of the Star of David for the North Star's representation, this version is one with its own legacy and invokes harmony and holy blessings in your home or rootwork.

Drunkards Path

This symbol was put out to recommend essentially a zigzag pattern of travel to the freedom seeker to thwart the efforts of slave hunters as well as hide certain tracks to safe locations. Most often it meant to travel south in plain sight, which rarely generated interest in bounty hunters, and head to the next location before doubling back north somewhere else not as heavily policed. The Drunkards Path is also an example of a code that has been utilized for a secondary purpose in conjure: to ward, sever, and uncross. This symbol was not only an indicator about direction of travel, but also a sigil for protection in general. It was and still is used to ward off, cut away, and uncross bad juju and malignant magic thrown your way. Placing it above a window or doorway on the outside or inside of your home will be effective. When doing so in whatever fashion you choose, be sure to take the time to work with the symbol, speaking aloud what you conjure it to do. Notice its sharp edges: like a knife or machete it will sever and cut negativity once you start to work with it.

Crossroads

In U.G.R.R. terminology Cleveland was called "crossroads" as well as "hope." This symbol, in particular in Ozella's quilt code, represented getting close to a renowned station, the last stop before freedom, that being Ohio and more specifically Cleveland. While this symbol can be used to adorn any part of your home as a station, a place to rest, as well as a place spirits can enter, for those that live in the Buckeye State or the greater Cleveland area, it can be a unique way to tie your home or ritual space into this legacy of a crossroads and place of hope. Cleveland's access to Lake Erie provided many routes that then went in different directions, and it was where many would be able to board a boat, with the next and final stop being southern Ontario.

The unique symbolism and geometric mysteries of the quilt codes capture the genius and art of the African American, who either utilized these symbols in secret codes to aid in a freedom break or created them as spiritual art and culture after the fact. As well, they represent another unique way that freedom seekers and their white allies worked together cloaked in esoteric mystery. Whichever way you choose to include them in your U.G.R.R. conjure, they will be excellent as beacons and warding for your magic with and for the spirits of the U.G.R.R. There are many more quilt codes. You can find entire books and poems about them. Some of them may speak to you and present themselves as useful or sacred symbols in your own work and research, helping you conjure, wield, and manifest with the spirits of the U.G.R.R.

The Nameless Followers, St. Catharines, circa 1850s, Rick Bell Family Fonds

Spirituals as Conjurations

In the consecration of our altar to Mama Moses, we recited or sang the spiritual "Go Down Moses." Many other spirituals also served as incantations and prayers that will please the spirits of the U.G.R.R. Once you begin to invoke and work with Mama Moses and her Followers more often, inserting any of the spirituals as incantations and callings will make the connection that much more tangible. They can be recited, sung, or whispered, whether at the altar, during work with the spirits, or while outside in nature—in your own region or at historic locations associated with the U.G.R.R. Mama Moses loved spirituals. She used them on her tracks as codes and signals and loved to sing in general. But she also composed her own.

When enlisting spirituals as incantations and conjurations for the spirits, it helps to light a taper or jar candle and hold it while intoning them. This step brings illumination, focus, and sanctity to your work and conjures. As with any invocation to Mama Moses or her Followers, knocking or lightly stomping three times just beforehand is an effective means to announce yourself and enhance the connection. The spirituals reveal but a glimpse of the genius, magic, and devotion of those that were in bondage and their will to survive and be free. To recite or sing them will bring the spirits comfort, and at times you will feel or hear them join you in sacred song.

"When the Chariot Comes"

Mama Moses sang this spiritual aloud on the plantation the night before she made history and fled for freedom, setting in motion her fate that would in turn intertwine with the fates of countless for generations to come. The allegory is rich and for the most part self-explanatory: leaving friends and loved ones behind, crossing the River Jordan, bound for the Promised Land. This spiritual, when sung, recited, or whispered, will make the spirit of Mama Moses happy, as well as her Followers.

When that old chariot comes,

I'm going to leave you,

I'm bound for the promised land,

Friends, I'm going to leave you.

I'm sorry, friends, to leave you,

Farewell! Oh, farewell!

But I'll meet you in the morning,

Farewell! Oh, farewell!

I'll meet you in the morning,

When I reach the promised land;

On the other side of Jordan,

For I'm bound for the promised land.

"Hail, Oh Hail Ye Happy Spirits"

Harriet Tubman composed her own spirituals, and this was one she sang to those hiding in a safe spot till she returned with provisions and/or news. She would arrive back at the hiding spots at nightfall and sing this spiritual twice if it was safe to come out and continue. In her own words, she described it this way: "The first time I go by singing this hymn, they don't come out to me . . . till I listen if the coast is clear, then when I go back and sing it again, they come out."

Hail, oh hail ye happy spirits,

death no more shall make you fear.

No grief, no sorrow, no pain, no anguish

shall no more distress you there.

Around him are ten thousand angels

always ready to obey command.

They are always hovering round you,

till you reach the heavenly land.

Jesus, Jesus will go with you;

he will lead you to his throne.

He who died has gone before you

trod the wine press all alone.

He whose thunder shakes creation,

he who bids the planets roll,

He who rides above the temple,

and his sceptre sways the whole.

Dark and thorny is the desert,

Through the pilgrim makes his ways,

Yet beyond this vale of sorrow

Lies the fields of endless days.

"Swing Low, Sweet Chariot"

Mama Moses's favorite hymn was "Swing Low, Sweet Chariot." Anytime you see fit, reciting or singing this spiritual will bring her joy as well as act as a call or invocation. She loved its symbolism taken from Exodus, featuring Elijah, Ezekiel, and the blazing chariot that takes them to a just glory.

I looked over Jordan and what did I see?

(Coming for to carry me home)

A band of angels coming after me

(Coming for to carry me home)

Swing low, sweet chariot

(Coming for to carry me home)

Swing low, sweet chariot

(Coming for to carry me home)

If you get there before I do

(Coming for to carry me home),

Tell all of my friends, that I'm coming there too

(Coming for to carry me home)

Swing low, sweet chariot,

Coming for to carry me home.

Swing low, sweet chariot,

Coming for to carry me home.

"Wade in the Water"

This spiritual told escaping slaves to get off the land trail and into the water. Wading in water would avoid leaving a scent that dogs could follow, dumbing the hounds that slave catchers used to sniff out and track their trail.

Who are those children all dressed in Red?

God's gonna trouble the water.

Must be the ones that Moses led.

God's gonna trouble the water.

    Chorus: *Wade in the Water, wade in the water, children.*

    Wade in the Water. God's gonna trouble the water.

Who are those children all dressed in White?

God's gonna trouble the water.

Must be the ones of the Israelites.

God's gonna trouble the water.

    Chorus.

Who are those children all dressed in Blue?

God's gonna trouble the water.

Must be the ones that made it through.

God's gonna trouble the water.

Chorus.

"*Steal Away*"

"Steal Away" was sung to signal to those in the know or who were prepared to embark on their journey and "steal away" that the freedom train would soon begin to roll.

My Lord calls me!

He calls me by the thunder!

The trumpet sounds it ina my soul!

I ain't got long to stay here!

Chorus: *Steal away, steal away!*

Steal away to Jesus!

Steal away, steal away home!

I ain't got long to stay here!

My Lord, he calls me!

He calls me by the lightning!

The trumpet sounds it ina my soul!

I ain't got long to stay here!

Chorus.

"Come Ride"

The spiritual "Come Ride" is a more modern one, arriving circa 2003. This spiritual is one of the ones shared by the Niagara Voodoo Shrine and sung at public ceremonies, festivals, gatherings, and cultural events and especially when we build and consecrate a Cairn and Cross. It is very familiar to Mama Moses and the spirits of the U.G.R.R.

Come ride, this train

Come walk, to freedom

Come ride, this train

With me

Praise be Harriet Tubman, Spirit of the night

Shotgun in hand, your freedom in sight

"Follow the Drinking Gourd"

There is some debate as to whether this spiritual was sung among the freedom seekers in the days of the U.G.R.R. or as an inspirational homage after emancipation. While it is most likely a folk song and spiritual created after the U.G.R.R. tracks ceased to be used, it matters not. "Follow the Drinking Gourd" is a potent and sacred testament to the means and ways of the Underground Railroad. It houses many of the mysteries of coded song and innuendo, signs of nature and landmarks that pointed to the path to freedom. It is homage to the trails that started in Mobile,

Alabama, and refers to the landmarks and natural signposts followed on foot up through Tennessee and Ohio, crossing waterways all the way to Canada. It makes reference to an individual or "folk hero" and spirit called "Peg Leg Joe." There were a host of "Peglegs" along the trails to freedom, associated with river crossings and navigators of the waters. This spiritual notes the seasonal migrations of birds and changes of weather, all interconnected into a sacred testament of the coded spiritual.

When the Sun comes back

And the first quail calls,

Follow the drinking gourd.

For the old man is a-waiting for to carry you to freedom

If you follow the drinking gourd.

The riverbank makes a very good road.

The dead trees will show you the way.

Left foot, peg foot, traveling on,

Follow the drinking gourd.

The river ends between two hills,

Follow the drinking gourd.

There's another river on the other side,

Follow the drinking gourd.

When the great big river meets the little river,

Follow the drinking gourd.

For the old man is a-waiting for to carry to freedom

If you follow the drinking gourd.

Liberty or Death: A Sonnet for Harriet by Rainbow Zetwal

I feared her near as much as I feared chains

this vessel of the lords holiest light

for freedom's fire boiled within her veins

and it lit the lamp through slavery's long dark night

through swamp and snow, through weariness and weather

we'd long since passed the point of no return

this tiny woman held us all together

and with the light of freedom made us burn

with bare and wounded feet I walked those roads

I'm shamed to say I tired and tried to balk

but I had seen the Quakers and the codes

she could not take the chance that I would talk

she cocked her pistol, aimed it at my head

and "you'll be free or die right here" she said

Spirit Dancing

My ancestors rejoice strongly all around me.

I can hear them breathing.

I can hear them praying.

I can feel their presence.

I know they are there, for I am aware.

—Anonymous, this poem hangs on the walls of the BME Church

Bibliography

Adler, David A. *Harriet Tubman and the Underground Railroad*. New York: Holiday House, 2013.

Anderson, Jeffrey E. *Conjure in African American Society*. Baton Rouge: Louisiana State University Press, 2005

Benét, Stephen Vincent. *John Brown's Body*. New York: Book of the Month Club, 1980.

Bennett, Lerone, Jr. *Before the Mayflower: A History of Black America*. Chicago: Johnson Pub. Co., 1969.

Bibbs, Susheel. *Heritage of Power*. Berkeley: MEP Productions, 1998.

Blockson, Charles L. *Hippocrene Guide to the Underground Railroad*. New York: Hippocrene Books, 1994.

Bordewich, Fergus. *Bound for Canaan: The Underground Railroad and the War for the Soul of America*. New York: Amistad, 2005.

Botkin, B. A., ed. *Lay My Burden Down: A Folk History of Slavery*. Chicago: University of Chicago Press, 1945.

Bradford, Sarah. *Harriet Tubman: The "Moses of Her People."* New York: J. J. Little Co., 1901.

Bradford, Sarah. *Scenes in the Life of Harriet Tubman*. Freeport, N.Y.: Books for Libraries Press, 1971.

Clinton, Catherine. *Harriet Tubman: The Road to Freedom*. Boston: Little, Brown, 2004.

Conrad, Earl. *Harriet Tubman: Negro Soldier and Abolitionist*. New York: International Publishers, 1942.

DeCaro, Jr., Louis A. *"Fire from the Midst of You": A Religious Life of John Brown*. New York: New York University Press, 2004.

Douglass, Frederick. *My Bondage and My Freedom*. New York: Penguin Books, 2003.

Douglass, Frederick. *Narrative of the Life of Frederick Douglass, an American Slave*. New York: Laurel, 1997.

Doyle, Arthur Conan. *The History of Spiritualism*. London: Cassel, 1926.

Drew, Benjamin. *The Refugees: The Narratives of Fugitive Slaves in Canada*. Toronto: Dundurn Press, 2008.

Du Bois, W. E. B. *John Brown, A Biography*. Armonk, N.Y.: M.E. Sharpe, 1997.

Elkins, Stanley. *Slavery: A Problem in American Institutional and Intellectual Life*. New York: Universal Library, 1963.

Eskridge, Ann E. *Slave Uprisings and Runaways: Fighting for Freedom and the Underground Railroad*. Berkeley Heights, N.J.: Enslow, 2004.

Federal Writers' Project. Alabama Slave Narratives.

Federal Writers' Project. Arkansas Slave Narratives.

Federal Writers' Project. Georgia Slave Narratives.

Federal Writers' Project. North Carolina Slave Narratives.

Felder, Cain Hope, ed. *Stony the Road We Trod, African American Biblical Interpretation*. Minneapolis: Fortress Press, 1991.

Foner, Eric. *Gateway to Freedom: The Hidden History of the Underground Railroad*. New York: Norton, 2015.

Foxwood, Orion. *The Candle and the Crossroads: A Book of Appalachian Conjure and Southern Root Work*. San Francisco: Weiser Books, 2012.

Frost, Karolyn Smardz. *I've Got a Home in Glory Land: A Lost Tale of the Underground Railroad*. Toronto: Thomas Allen, 2007.

Fry, Gladys-Marie. *Stitched from the Soul: Slave Quilts from the Antebellum South.* Chapel Hill: University of North Carolina Press, 2002.

Furnas, J. C. *The Road to Harpers Ferry.* New York: W. Sloane Associates, 1959.

Gates, Henry Louis, Jr., ed. *The Classic Slave Narratives.* New York: New American Library, 1987.

Glenelg. *Broken Shackles: Old Man Henson from Slavery to Freedom.* Toronto: Natural Heritage Books, 2001.

Grant, R. G. *Slavery: Real People and Their Stories of Enslavement.* New York: DK Pub, 2009.

Hendrix, John. *John Brown: His Fight for Freedom.* New York: Abrams, 2009.

Henson, Josiah. *The Life of Josiah Henson, Formerly a Slave, Now an Inhabitant of Canada.* Boston: Arthur D. Phelps, 1849.

Hill, Daniel G. *The Freedom-Seekers: Blacks in Early Canada.* Toronto: Stoddart, 1992.

Hudson, Lynn Maria. *The Making of "Mammy Pleasant": A Black Entrepreneur in Nineteenth-Century San Francisco.* Urbana: University of Illinois Press, 2003.

Humez, Jean McMahon. *Harriet Tubman: The Life and the Life Stories.* Madison: University of Wisconsin Press, 2003.

Hurmence, Belinda, ed. *Before Freedom: 48 Oral Histories of Former North and South Carolina Slaves.* Winston-Salem: J.F. Blair, 1989.

Larsen, Kate Clifford. *Bound for the Promised Land: Harriet Tubman, Portrait of an American Hero.* New York: Ballantine, 2004.

Laughlin-Schulz, Bonnie. *The Tie That Bound Us: The Women of John Brown's Family and the Legacy of Radical Abolitionism.* Ithaca: Cornell University Press, 2013.

McGowan, James A. *Station Master on the Underground Railroad: The Life and Letters of Thomas Garrett.* Jefferson, N.C.: McFarland & Co., 2005.

McGowan, James A., and William Kashatus. *Harriet Tubman: A Biography.* Santa Barbara, Calif.: ABC-CLIO, 2011.

McMullen, Stephanie. *From Slavery to Freedom: African Canadians in Grey County.* Owen Sound: County of Grey Museum, 2003.

McQuillar, Tayannah Lee. *Rootwork: Using the Folk Magick of Black America for Love, Money, and Success.* New York: Simon & Schuster, 2003.

Merrill, Arch. *The Underground, Freedom's Road, and Other Upstate Tales.* New York: American Book-Stratford Press, 1963.

Murphy, Lawrence R., and Ronnie C. Tyler, eds. *The Slave Narratives of Texas.* Austin: State House Press, 1997.

Northup, Solomon. *Twelve Years a Slave.* New York: Penguin, 2012.

Nudelman, Franny. *John Brown's Body: Slavery, Violence & the Culture of War.* Chapel Hill: University of North Carolina Press, 2004.

Oates, Stephen B. *To Purge This Land with Blood: A Biography of John Brown.* New York: Harper & Row, 1970.

Papson, Don, and Tom Calarco. *Secret Lives of the Underground Railroad in New York City: Sydney Howard Gay, Louis Napoleon and the Records of Fugitives.* Jefferson, N.C.: McFarland & Co., 2015.

Petitt, Eber M. *Sketches in the History of the Underground Railroad.* Fredonia, N.Y.: W. McKinstry & Son, 1879.

Pinckney, Roger. *Blue Roots: African American Folk Magic of the Gullah People.* Orangeburg, S.C.: Sandlapper, 2003.

Ramsey, Bets, and Merikay Waldvogel. *Southern Quilts: Surviving Relics of the Civil War.* Nashville: Rutledge Hill, 1998.

Roboteau, Albert J. *Slave Religion: The "Invisible Institution" in the Antebellum South.* New York: Oxford University Press, 2004.

Rupwate, Daniel D. *A Historical Significance of the "Salem Chapel" with Reference to the Underground Railroad*. Rt. Rev. Dr. Daniel D. Rupwate, 2005.

Sanborn, Franklin Benjamin. *The Life and Letters of John Brown: Liberator of Kansas and Martyr of Virginia*. Boston: Roberts Brothers, 1891.

Scott, Otto. *The Secret Six: John Brown and the Abolitionist Movement*. Murphys, Calif.: Uncommon Books, 1979.

Sernett, Milton. *Harriet Tubman: Myth, Memory, and History*. Durham, N.C.: Duke University Press, 2007.

Siebert, Wilbur Henry. *The Underground Railroad from Slavery to Freedom: A Comprehensive History*. Mineola, N.Y.: Dover, 2006.

Sterling, Dorothy. *Freedom Train: The Story of Harriet Tubman*. Garden City, N.Y.: Doubleday, 1954.

Switala, William J. *Underground Railroad in Pennsylvania*. Mechanicsburg, Penn.: Stackpole, 2008.

Thomas, Owen A. *Niagara's Freedom Trail: A Guide to African-Canadian History on the Niagara Peninsula*. Thorold, Ont.: Niagara Economic Development Corp., 2007.

Tobin, Jacqueline L., and Raymond G. Dobard. *Hidden in Plain View: The Secret Story of Quilts and the Underground Railroad*. New York: Doubleday, 1999.

Weatherford, Carole Boston. *Moses: When Harriet Tubman Led Her People to Freedom*. New York: Hyperion, 2006.

About the Author

Witchdoctor Utu is the founder of the world-renowned Pagan drum troupe the Dragon Ritual Drummers. He is the curator of the Niagara Voodoo Shrine, which is dedicated to Harriet "Mama Moses" Tubman and the spirits of the Underground Railroad, and is a member of the New Orleans Voodoo Spiritual Temple. For over twenty years, Utu has been active in both the American and Canadian Pagan and witchcraft communities and is a sought-after presenter. Since 2000, Utu has been immersed in the North American conjure, rootwork, and lore of the Underground Railroad. He resides in St. Catharines, Ontario, where Harriet Tubman brought her particular "tracks" to their end and where she planned and executed her many journeys for freedom. Utu has befriended scholars, clergy, and descendants of freedom seekers with knowledge of Mama Moses and the Underground Railroad few have access to. His work, magic, and teachings of conjure for Harriet Tubman and the spirits of the Underground Railroad are unprecedented.

To Our Readers

Weiser Books, an imprint of Red Wheel/Weiser, publishes books across the entire spectrum of occult, esoteric, speculative, and New Age subjects. Our mission is to publish quality books that will make a difference in people's lives without advocating any one particular path or field of study. We value the integrity, originality, and depth of knowledge of our authors.

Our readers are our most important resource, and we appreciate your input, suggestions, and ideas about what you would like to see published.

Visit our website at *www.redwheelweiser.com* to learn about our upcoming books and free downloads, and be sure to go to *www.redwheelweiser.com/newsletter* to sign up for newsletters and exclusive offers.

You can also contact us at *info@rwwbooks.com* or at

Red Wheel/Weiser, LLC
65 Parker Street, Suite 7
Newburyport, MA 01950